Undisclosed Facts
of Tribal Life

Undisclosed Facts of Tribal Life

Paramjot Singh Chahel

(Retd Judge.)

PARTRIDGE
A Penguin Random House Company

To order additional copies of this book, contact
Partridge India
000 800 10062 62
orders.india@partridgepublishing.com

www.partridgepublishing.com/india

Contents

Dedication

I dedicate this book to

S. PURAN SINGH KHANDA SINGH
KAMTHEKAR, (A martyr)

(He sacrificed his life in 1969, when there was a curfew
to control an incident of Ramayana)

Author Speaks

I was deputed as a Judge in the Court of Civil Judge at Dadra and Nagar Haveli at Silvassa. The Dadra and Nagar Haveli is beautiful Union Territory nestled amidst beautiful lush green hills, the starting point of western Ghats. The territory is rich in forest, river, animals, birds and impoverished Adivasi people. The territory has many Scheduled Tribe and caste known as Dhodia, Kathodi, Koli, Naykada and Varli. They have their unique family structure, the institution of marriage, divorce remarriage and religion. The forms of marriages prevalent among these tribes may surprise the urbanized people of other parts of the country.

I had an opportunity to decide the cases while hearing the argument from the members of the Bar Association, Silvassa. We both Judge and Advocates feel the need of document on longstanding customs. It enlightens me. I entered the central library, Silvassa. I have collected several reference books and made research. It concludes in, "Undisclosed Facts of Tribal Life" I have covered the tribal life. The ceremonies of child-birth, language taught to child, engagement and marriage custom. Pre-marital and extra marital sex relation, monogamy, polygamy, divorce culture and widow remarriage, status of GharJawai, ways of acquiring mates, food and drink, religion, God, Goddess, and vows to God, faith in medical profession etc.

I would like to summarize the survey report that child birth ceremony is known as "CHATTI". Their languages are Dhodia, Gujrati, Konkani, Marathi and Varli. The engagement and marriage custom performs by garlanding each other. Previously girl goes to the house of boy for marriage and stay there as known "UDHADI". They perform marriage in the day. They use bullock-cart for Barati. Now days it is replaced by motor vehicles. After marriage bride and bride-groom are separated by erecting separate hut near to their house. On next day to marriage bride is taken back to parent's home known as "AANU". In Gavit community children and parent perform their marriages at a time it is known "Nawara-Nawari" The engagement they refer as "Lagan nakki karyo", or "Chandala" or "Sakharpuda". In rare cases girl became mother first and then marry, as Naniben Patel told but nowadays the custom is not seen. There is no custom of extra martial sex relation. There is general practice of monogamy but there are rare cases of keeping two wives but not permitted in the existing law. Widows are allowed for re-marriage. The percentage of widow marriage in middle aged women is rare. The custom of GharJamai is called "Khandhadiya". It is called "service marriage". The ceremony called during pregnancy is known "Shrimant". Their food is bread. It is prepared by rice, jowar, makka, wheat, nagali. They eat shark, fish, and chicken. They drink Bear, mahuwa, tadi, desidaru. They used to dance toor-tarpa and thali. They believe in God Shankar, Swami Narayan, Brahdev, Ramdevgir, Konkani Maa and Pitrulok, Khwajagar, Nivaj, Mahalaxmi Mata. They wear

Kanchado and Blouce, Saree. Now a day it is noted that villagers are attracting towards Christian religion and Swami Narayan. They are performing the marriage as per Swami Narayan Religion. They are attending Church to get cloth and Ghamchha. They have extreme faith towards, baba, zhadfuk, bhagat if they are suffering from diseases. Nowadays, they are availing medical facilities from VinobaBhave Civil Hospital and private Doctors. Sometimes they scrummed to non-professional medical persons (Bhagat-Bhuva) and lost their lives.

- Paramjot Singh Chahel (Retd. Judge)

Gratitude

In support of literature, I have conducted local survey with the co-operation of Shri Kuldeep Singh, Director, Red Cross, Silvassa.

It's time to remember the helping hands and lovely touch to my work by Advocate Aditi Parida, B.A., L.L.M. I also extend my thanks to Mr. Harshadbhai Desai, Superintendent of central library, Silvassa for providing the study material. I cannot conclude without giving my thanks to Shri Bhavesh A. Shah, Mrs. Naincy Steno, Shri P.M. Shinde, Stenographer, Administration of Dadra and Nagar Haveli, Kishore Bhaidas Shirsath and Jitendra Dhodi. Hasmukh Bhai, Mihir Bhadsavle, Goutam.

It would be injustice to my research work if I conclude without providing special thanks to technocrat Delkar Mohan, Ex M.P., S.S.R. College, Silvassa. Shri Ajit Deshpande, Trustee, Eminent Professors Dr. Rajeshwari Nair, Vice Principal and Prof. Dr. Minaxshi, HOD of Dept. of Psychology.

Finally, I pen off by expressing my deep gratitude to Satpal Singh Gill, a Guide in Career Guidance Annual Camp organized by Navjyot Foundation, Nanded and Author of G-Thoughts (Vol. 1) "No Sunrise without Sunset", for helping me in editing and topic arrangement of the book.

Applaud

Justice A. V. Nirgude

10, High Court Campus,
Jalna Road,
Aurangabad 431005
Ph. 0240-2486676

15th December, 2014
Aurangabad

M E S S A G E

Shri Paramjot Singh Chahel is my childhood friend. Besides being a Judicial Officer, he has nurtured writing as hobby quite seriously. He has written several books after undertaking painstaking research on the subjects. This book which he started writing during his last year of service as Judicial Officer is written after collecting data on habits and habitats of tribal people in India.

As usual Paramjot researched the subject for describing in his lucid way the lifestyle of tribal people including their food habits, social etiquettes, faith and religious rituals etc.

I appreciated more the part of the book where he has pointed out detrimental effects on their life due to their gross credulity and superstition. He also studied and described unique problems faced by women during old age, pregnancy, childbirth, matrimonial relationships, widowhood etc.

I wish him well and hope that he would continue writing in his retired life.

[Justice A.V. Nirgude]
Judge, Bombay High Court
Bench at Aurangabad

NATUBHAI G. PATEL
Member of Parliament, Lok Sabha
Dadra & Nagar Haveli (U.T.)
Member:
* Standing Committee on Home
* Consultative Committee on Finance

Office: Plot No. 31, Yogi Sadan
Vapi Road, Silvassa
Dadra & Nagar Haveli-396230
Phone: 0260-2633000, 2633900
Fax: 0260-2632905
E-mail: yogisilvassa@rediffmail.com

Residence: 113, South Avenue
New Delhi-110011
Phone: 011-23795358

Date: 05/09/2014

MESSAGE

I am delighted to go through the book, **"Undisclosed Facts of Tribal Life"** written by the Shri. Paramjot Singh Chahel, Ex- Chief Judicial Magistrate and Civil Judge Sr. Division of Dadra & Nagar Haveli, Silvassa. The book describes the custom and traditions of various tribes in India, particularly some of those inhabit the Union Territory of Dadra & Nagar Haveli.

I wish the publication all success and hope that he should devote his time in academic vocation.

With Regards

[Natubhai Patel]

भूपिन्द्र एस. भल्ला, भा.प्र.से.
Bhupinder S. Bhalla, IAS
प्रशासक
ADMINISTRATOR

संघ प्रदेश दमण एवं दीव और
दादरा एवं नगर हवेली,
सचिवालय, मोटी दमण-३६६, २२०
Union Territories of Daman & Diu
and Dadra & Nagar Haveli,
Secretariat, Moti Daman, Daman-396 220
Tel.: (0260) 2230700 / 2230770 / 264277?
FAX : (0260) 2230735 / 2642702
Email : administrator-dd-dnh@nic.in

I am delighted to go through the book "Undisclosed Facts of Tribal Life" penned by Shri Paramjot Singh Chahal, Ex-Chief Judicial Magistrate of Dadra & Nagar Haveli. The book describes the customs and traditions of various tribes in India, particularly some of those that inhabit the Union Territory of Dadra & Nagar Haveli. I am sure that the work would be useful for anthropologists and general readers alike.

I wish the publication all success and hope that Shri Chahal continues to utilize his spare time for academic pursuits.

(Bhupinder S. Bhalla)
Administrator

April 30, 2013

"Undisclosed Facts of Tribal Life" is book written by our beloved Paramjot Singh Chahel, retired judge of civil court of Dadara and Nagar Haveli Silvassa. He has taken keen interest and searched valuable pearls from the fathom of tribes and their life, culture, habit and habitats. I always remember his work and devotion towards the mankind while he was working on Dais.

I wish he shall utilize the time in social work.

Shri Jawahar Desai
Advocate, Vapi Gujrat

The collection of my colleague is nothing but disclosure of facts which are important to be known to the people of that tribes also. It would be assets to the students and teachers to know the caste, tribes, and their rituals of birth, marriage, divorce, remarriage, widows, the misunderstanding about sex before marriage and after marriage, death and concerned ceremonies are elaborated with reference books, are marvelous and hard work.

Shri Rakshe
Advocate, and Judge Retd.,
Daman U.T.

The task carried by the Paramjot Singh Chahel, then Civil Judge Silvassa, author of this book, is valuable in its own nature. He has taken pain and deep interest in study of tribal life is admirable and creates new effects of actual custom prevails in tribal cost. The details and the reliance placed by this book will certainly helpful to all concern not only for academic requirement but also for the facts, which are not generally known to the public at large. The custom is always difficult to prove but its strength shall affect more to the rights of tribal.

I wish all success to such immense work.

Shri K. M. Brahambhatt
Advocate, VAPI

Author wrote a book because he is in a habit of reading and writing. I myself compel to extend heartiest thanks to him of selecting the subject touching to the various caste and tribes of Silvassa area in particular and India in general. He has disclosed the various aspects which are unknown to the natives.

All my best wishes to him and his work.

Shri D.G. Shaha
Advocate, Silvassa

Connotation of 'Tribe'

Tribe, caste, sect and class are the various categories of social stratification found in India. A 'tribe' is a collection of families or groups of families, bearing a common name, members of which occupy the same territory, speaks the same language and observe certain taboos regarding marriage, profession or occupation and have developed a well assessed system of reciprocity and mutuality of obligations. A tribe is ordinarily an endogamous unit, the members of which confine their marriage within the tribe. Several clans constitute a tribe, each of which claims kinship between the members belonging to it, based either on totalistic division, territorial contiguity or common residence. A tribe is a political unit in the sense that the tribal society owns a political organization; either recognizes hereditary tribal chiefs or the several sections of it are welded into a territorial group rule over by class chiefs of hereditary kings.

'Tribe', 'caste', 'sect' and 'class' are used synonymously and therefore, many castes are described as tribe and many tribes have been described as 'caste'. It is a difficult job to separate social groups as 'castes' and 'tribe'.

Some sociologists and anthropologists define tribes as social groups speaking a common dialect. W. J. Perry observes ... "tribe is a group speaking a common dialect and inhabiting a common territory."

Marriage

The institution of marriage is another point on which the tribal people throughout the world have been much maligned. Wild and baseless charges were hurled at them, fantastic insinuations were formulated and many pseudo-scholars, claiming to have an intimate knowledge of the tribal world, let their imagination run riot for the benefit of a receptive readership. Some degree of laxity regarding sexual liaison was taken to mean 'promiscuity' or free sex under which, according to such people, the institution of marriage could not exist. Such spicy phrases like 'sexual communism' were coined to describe a non-existent social situation. Indian tribes like tribes of other parts of the world practice several forms of marriage as a matter of convenience and social acclimatization in their respective cultural-ecological settings.

Monogamy

Monogamy is a form of marriage in which no man may be married to more than one woman at any one time. A majority of the Indian tribes practice monogamy. Just to refute the allegation that among the most backward and primitive tribes no clear-cut scheme of marriage exists, the example of the Kamar, a very backward tribe of Madhya Pradesh, may be cited. This tribe is monogamous.

Polygamy

Polygamy, that is, marriage to more than one person is fairly widespread all over the world. Among Indian tribes, there are many who are following this type of matrimonial alliance. Polygamy has two aspects:

i.   Polygyny
ii. Polyandry.

While polygyny is the marriage of one man to several women, polyandry means the marriage of one woman to several men. Both types of marriages are referred to as polygamy in common parlance.

Polygyny is found among the Naga tribes, the Gond, the Baiga, the Toda, the Lushai and most of the other Proto-Australoid tribes of middle India. In most cases such form of marriage comes into existence as a result of disequilibrium in a sex ratio. Obviously, in a society where the sex ratio is normal, such type of marriage may force many of the male members to remain bachelor. Hence, normally such a practice develops in a society where the number of females is quite larger than the males. In an otherwise normal situation it is the privilege of the powerful and rich who keep more than one wife as a symbol of prestige and status. Among the Indian tribes like Gond, Baiga and Lushai, this type of marriage is resorted to, facilitate a better division of labour. Polyandry is, comparatively, much restricted in distribution. This type of matrimonial alliance is found in the Himalayan tract stretching from Kashmir to Assam and is popular among the Indo-Aryan and Mongoloid tribes. In its classical form it is prevalent among the Tiyan, the Toda, the Kota, the Khasa (Jounsari) and the Kadakhi Bota. It is also popular among the Tibetans.

Among the Indian tribes, two types of polyandry are in vogue. When several brothers share the same wife, as among the Khasa and the Toda, we have fraternal polyandry. Majumdar (1967) opines that in the general type, also found among the Toda of Nilgiri Hills, there need not be any close relationship between the husbands, and the wife goes to spend some time with each husband. So long as a woman lives with one of her husbands, the others have no claim over her. Nayar polyandry was of this type. Polyandry is not everywhere explicable with reference to a preponderance of men over women. In Ladakh it was actually the women who were more in number. Among the Toda, property considerations and sex- disparity explain this institution. Polyandry is found to lead to fewer children to every woman, more male children, and a high incidence of sterility among women.

The Khasa have evolved a very practical mode of polyandrous matrimony. Among them, when the eldest brother marries a girl, she automatically becomes the common wife of the rest of the brothers. If a brother is minor, he may, on becoming adult, marry another girl to match his age. Hence this leads to a situation where a number of brothers have more than one wife which is not the classical mode of polyandry. Observing polygyny and polyandry mixed up, Majumdar coined an interesting phrase, Polyandry, to describe this situation.

Till some time back the Todas of Nilgiri Hills used to observe an interesting ceremony called bow and arrow ceremony to declare the paternity socially. In this ceremony, all brothers and the common wife assemble amidst the rest of the villagers in the fourth or fifth month of pregnancy of the wife and as a result of consensus one of the brothers presents a set of bow and arrow to the wife. This is taken as declaration that this particular brother will be accepted as father of the coming child. In this way 'sociological fatherhood' overrides the 'biological fatherhood' in the bewildering mosaic of human affairs.

Beside demographic factors, an economic factor called bride price is also responsible for the prevalence of polyandry among Indian tribes. Under the system of bride price the husband/husbands are obliged to give an agreed amount of cash/kind to the parents of the bride as price which usually varies according to the physical beauty and utility of the bride. With the passage of time the bride price continued to soar and a stage came when it became almost impossible to arrange the bride price individually. Furthermore, the agricultural holdings in mountains are quite uneconomic and the pursuit of cultivation too hard to be borne by a single individual. Hence, to avoid further fragmentation of holdings and sharing the enormous labour, such a mode of marriage might have come into existence.

Another mode of polygamy, which may be called 'bigamy', is also in vogue, though on a very restricted scale. Under bigamy a man is allowed to marry two sisters at one time. This type of polygamy has been reported from the Holiya and Medara tribes.

Preferential Marriage and Prohibitions

It is observed that, on the one hand, the society prohibits sexual liaison or matrimonial alliances between particular kins or in the same clan or gotra but on the other hand, it encourages, matrimonial alliances between certain other kins. In such cases there is a prescription, or only a preference, expressed for marriage to a particular kin. The following are some of the popular types of 'preferential' marriages prevalent among the Indian tribes:

1. Cousin marriage
   a. cross-cousin marriage
   b. parallel-cousin marriage
2. Levirate
3. Soro rate

Both types of cousin marriage, viz. cross-cousin marriage are quite popular among the Indian tribes. The Gond, Kharia, Khasi and Nadar are some of the important Indian tribes practicing cousin marriage. Anthropologically speaking, when the children of a brother and a sister marry, it is a cross-cousin marriage while it is parallel cousin marriage when the children of two sisters or two brothers get married. A Gond is supposed to marry his or her cross cousin, and if one likes to have this prescription waived in one's case, compensation has to be paid to the losing party. Cross-cousin marriage, as observed by Majumdar, is. The Gonds of Madhya Pradesh call this form of marriage 'Doodh Lautawa' (return of milk). The implication is that the bride price paid by 'A' for his wife would be returned to his family when the daughter of 'A' marries her mother's brother's son. Claude Levi Strauss has said that preferential marriage has, for its main purpose, the strengthening of solidarity within a tribe.

Levirate and sororate are two other types of preferential marriages which are also said to promote 'inter-familial cordiality' by making certain linkages imperative. When a woman marries her husband's brother this is called levirate. It may be split into two types: (a) junior levirate, (b) senior levirate. When the woman marries her husband's younger brother, it is junior levirate while marriage with the elder brother is called senior levirate. When levirate occurs in non-polyandrous societies, it is of paramount importance because in the event of her husband's death, the widow finds a guardian, husband and patron while the children get a man as their father who has loved them earlier too. Among some tribal groups, a degree of laxity is allowed in the matter of intimate social relations and sexual liaison between a woman and her husband's brothers as a prelude to the coming event. This situation may be termed as 'anticipatory levirate'!

When a man marries his wife's sister/sisters, it is sororate. It may occur after the death of his wife or even in her life. The death of a spouse is compensated by supplying a new spouse, generally a younger sister of the deceased. Levirate and sororate emphasize the acceptance of inter-familial obligations and the recognition of marriage as a tie between two families, and not only between two individuals.

Ways of Acquiring Mates

Nine important ways of acquiring a mate have been found to be popular among the Indian tribes:

1. Marriage by capture
2. Marriage by exchange
3. Marriage by purchase
4. Marriage by elopement
5. Marriage by service
6. Marriage by intrusion
7. Marriage by trial
8. Marriage by mutual consent
9. Marriage by probation.

When a man forcibly snatches away a woman from her village and marries her, it is called marriage by 'capture'. Many tribal societies give social sanction to this type of marriage which symbolizes velour and chivalry. Marriage by capture has been most popular among the Naga tribes of north eastern region where Naga tribal of one village used to invade the enemy's village and capture grown up girls. This led to female infanticide. However, with the widening application of the Indian Penal Code and growing social consciousness as a result of culture contacts this practice is fast vanishing into oblivion. Among some other tribes like Bhumij, Kharia, Munda, Santhals etc., this practice has given place to mock capture as a 'survival' of the old practice in which after finalizing the marriage the parents of the girl request the groom to come to an agreed place and 'capture their daughter'. In a mock gesture, the girl (bride) also puts on symbolic resistance. Among some tribes like Ho, it is the exorbitant rate of bride price that often leads to marriage by capture.

Majumdar reports that in Assam, physical captures take place during raids by one village on another. In middle India, the methodic more peaceful, capture being effected on festival days at inter- village meets when there is much rivalry, drinking and intoxication. Such captures are given social sanction by requiring the gallant who has made the capture to pay compensation and/or give a feast to the tribal brotherhood.

Marriage by exchange has primarily been evolved as a means of avoiding the payment of high bride price. Under such a marriage two households exchange women with each other and thus avoid the payment of bride price. This practice is found, in varying degrees, all over India in which a man gives his sister or any other woman of his household in exchange of his wife. Interestingly, the Khasi tribals of Meghalaya do not permit it.

Marriage by the 'purchase' is a highly prevalent mode of matrimony throughout tribal India. Bride price is the central theme in this type of marriage. This is paid either in cash or in kind or partly in cash and partly in kind. Lowie has emphasized that although the economic nature of this transaction cannot be minimized, it nevertheless would be wrong to regard the payment of a bride price as indicating sale and purchase. It may be only symbolic of the utility of a woman, and by way of compensation to her parent's family. Among the major tribes, marriage by payment of bride price is prevalent among the Munda, Oraon, Ho, Santhal, Rengma Naga, etc. The worst consequences of bride price are probably seen among the Ho tribal of Chotanagpur, Bihar. Their poor general economic condition has been made worst by the ever increasing amount of bride price. The amount is so high, and to accept a lower amount being against one's status and prestige, that many young men and women remain unmarried. These unfortunate young men often resort to marriage by capture and the spinsters have often to undergo further injustice by being identified with witchcraft and sorcery. In many cases their natural desire to marry leads them into the clutches of the cunning moneylenders and the consequent bondedness.

Marriage by elopement is also a peculiar feature of tribal in India. As is well-known, child marriage is a new phenomenon in tribal India. They started adopting it as a result of culture contact with their Hindu neighborhood. Previously, only adults entered into married life, and therefore, almost everywhere, marriage by mutual consent with parents' approval was the general rule. But with the changing times boys and girls started shedding their traditional submissiveness. In case the parents' consent is not forthcoming, an elopement is generally the way out. Of course, the indulgent elders receive back the over fond couple. This practice is often resorted to in the face of high bride price. The tribes of Chotanagpur are famous for one type of elopement or the other.

Marriage by 'service' is another way of avoiding the payment of bride price altogether or minimizing it considerably through service rendered by the prospective groom at bride's residence. Thus, if a Gond or Baiga finds himself not in a position to pay the bride price, he goes to serve in his would-be father-in-law's house as a suitor servant and marries the desired girls after a lapse of some years. Purum of Manipur recognizes it as the only traditionally genuine mode of matrimony. They have to work in the bride's household for three years and have to fulfill all the responsibilities of a son. The boarding and lodging arrangements are taken care of by the would-be-in laws during the entire period of stay. Among the Birhor, the father-in-law often lends money, which is returned in installments to enable the son-in-law to pay the bride price. Till such time as the loan is repaid, the son-in-law is compelled to stay at his father-in-law's household.

The opposite of 'marriage by capture' is also found among the Indian tribes and is known as 'marriage by intrusion'. This is the case of a girl desirous of marrying an unwilling young man. In such a case the girl thrust herself on the unwilling groom and his parents. She tries to serve the 'would be man' in his life and his parents but is humiliated and tortured in return. If she persists in her intentions and her endurance lasts for a considerable period she is finally accepted as daughter-in-law of the household. The Birhor and the Ho of Chotanagpur are some of the major tribes who practice it. Ho calls it, very appropriately, ***anadar,*** meaning humiliation or disrespect.

Marriage by 'trial' is another way of acquiring mate among some of the Indian tribes. It is the recognition of personal courage and bravery as highly desirable traits in a Youngman. The prospective groom has to prove his prowess before he can claim the hand of the desired girl. It is most popular among the Bhil. During the Holi festival young men and women perform a folk dance round a pole or a tree to the top of which a ***coconut*** and ***gur*** are tied. All the young men and women are free to participate in the dance, locally called a ***'gol gadedho'***. The girls make an inner ring of dancers round the tree. When a young man attempts to break through the cordon to climb the tree to eat the gur and break open coconut, the girls resist his attempt with their full force. The aspirant may incur even severe injuries but it is taken in good faith. If in spite of these obstacles, a daring man succeeds in this drama, he has the right to demand any of the surrounding girls as his wife.

Marriage by 'mutual consent' is the result of the tribals' contact with the Hindus. This practice is similar to that prevalent among the Muslims, Hindus, Christians, etc., in which all the formalities of marriage are arranged by the parties concerned through the process of mutual consultation and consent.

Probationary marriage can be called as primitive version of modern practice of courtship before marriage. Under this practice the prospective husband and wife are permitted to live together for some time in the bride's house. If they like each other and decide to marry, elders arrange their early marriage. In case the couple do not find each other's temperament to be suitable and compatible they separate and the man has to pay cash compensation to the girl's parents. Such a practice is widely prevalent among the Kuki of Arunachal Pradesh. Some tribal groups of Chotanagpur also approve of this practice and call it ***Raazi-Khushi***.

Pre-marital and Extra-marital Sex Relations

This is another area of tribal life which has been shamelessly exploited by many authors and journalists who have tried to enter into overnight fame by un-thoughtful and exaggerated versions of the tribals' pre-marital and extra-marital sex life. When the imagination of others run riot, it is to the anthropologist's credit that skillfully avoids these pitfalls and makes a serious and objective study of all the aspects of tribal life, including his sex life.

Pre-marital sex relations, in varying degrees, are seen to be permissible all over tribal India, as with the tribal people of other parts of the world. Obviously the conception of virginity or chastity in a society plays the crucial role in this context.

Among the tribes of middle India, pre-marital sex relations are overlooked unless of course they lead to pregnancy which is generally regarded as shameful for the girl's parents. Also, for a girl to become pregnant is regarded as an extreme family disgrace. She is asked to name the child's father and he is forced to marry her. In this case the amount of bride price is either reduced considerably or it is waived altogether. Among the Koinyak Naga, the girl continues to live in her parent's house even after marriage where her conduct is overlooked by the parents and other village people. Usually after the birth of her first child, she moves to her husband's household. Among the Muria Gond of Bastar, young boys and girls are traditionally allowed a degree of permissiveness within the four walls of the youth dormitory. All the stages of courtship are gone through and they get married with the blessings and approval of their parents. Also Naga too, does not attach undue importance to the so-called virginity of the girls.

Extra-marital sex relations are not as common or permissible as pre-marital liaison. It has been reported that among the Maria, the main cause of high incidence of murder and suicide has been marital infidelity. But the Tharu tribe of Uttar Pradesh presents an interesting spectacle. The Tharu men are said to be so much overwhelmed and overawed by the beauty of their wives that they play only second fiddle to them. The wife may indulge in extramarital sexual liaison and get away with it.

The Khasa or Jaunsari tribe of Uttar Pradesh has evolved a different value system regarding the extra-marital sex relations. Since most of the girls are married off at an early age, there is hardly any possibility of pre-marital liaison. Hence, their main worry is about extra marital relations. In her parental house, the wife is called *dhanti,* while in her husband's house she is called *rhanti*. These two seemingly ordinary words of native dialect carry a very significant connotation. When she is dhanti, a woman enjoys all sorts of freedom. She is a free bird. She can meet anybody. Allow anybody to take liberties with her. But the same woman is like a chained slave while she is rhanti. In her husband's house she has to work hard in the fields and in the house; she is generally frustrated and her conduct and movement always remain under the strict control of her husband/husbands and other affine relations. For a little respite, she comes to her parents' house generally during local fairs and festivals. The strains which these women suffer by being wife to several men, who are mentally and physically unlike each other, are relieved by the unfettered life which she can lead in her parents' village.

This sort of dual role prompted some anthropologists and sociologists like Majumdar (1962) and Saxena (1964) to term it as *"dual morality"* which is quite a misnomer when viewed by an outsider who tries to measure the moral fabric of these simple folk with his own yardstick of puritan hypocrisy and so-called morality.

Divorce

Unlike Hindus, marriage is not a religious sacrament among the tribes of India. Hence, divorce or dissolution of marriage is not only possible but widely practiced. It may easily be obtained if the parties no longer wish to live in wedlock.

The ground for divorce, however, varies from tribe to tribe. The Khasis permit divorce for reasons of adultery, barrenness and incompatibility of temperament. In some cases, the party desiring the dissolution may have to pay compensation to the other party and remarriage between such people is not possible. The divorce, like marriage, has to be a public ceremony where the mother gets the custody of the children. The Lushai, however, allow remarriage between those once divorced. The Gond, Kharia and others also allow divorce freely on grounds of marital infidelity, sterility, laziness, etc.

Despite contacts with the Hindus, widow remarriage is still practiced among almost all the tribes of India and there is little likelihood of its discontinuation since widow remarriage carries on stigma among the Indian tribes the plight of a young woman falling widow is far from miserable.

References

1. Pande G C Economic Development Planning in India Vol II Anmol Publishers New Delhi 1978.
2. Pande G C Travails of Tribal Change Ed Hunalaa and Development Journal of H R G S C Joshi et al Nainital 1980 No2.

Dhodia

It is believed that the term Dhodia has been derived from Dhulia, a place in Maharashtra, from where two Rajput princes came to Gujarat and married two Naika women. Another legend traces their origin to Dholuka-Dhandhuh, a place near the south bank of the Narmada river. It is also said that they are Jadhav Rajputs, descendants of Lord Krishna. Enthoven (1920) writes that the Dhodia are one of the largest early tribes who chiefly work as field laborers and hereditary servants. The Dhodia are mainly distributed in the Surat and Valsad districts of Gujarat. The area inhabited by them is a hilly terrain surrounded by dry deciduous forests. The population of this community is 449,130 (1981 census), a considerable percentage of which (11.42 per cent) is returned from urban areas. Their mother tongue, Dhodia, belongs to the Bhili group of the Indo-Aryan family of languages. The Gujarati language is used for inter-group communication and they use the Gujarati script.

The Dhodia are divided into a number of equally ranked exogamous clans. Enthoven (1920) has identified several exogamous kuls. They are monogamous and their marriages are generally fixed through negotiation. The symbols of marriage are the vermilion mark *(kanku)* and a necklace *(mangalsutra)*. Bride price is paid. The rule of residence after marriage is patriarch. Divorce and remarriage are permitted and a widow may marry her late husband's younger brother while a widower is allowed to marry his deceased wife's younger sister. Both extended and nuclear families are found in this community. Parental property is divided equally among the sons and the eldest son succeeds his father after his death. Women work in different agricultural operations, collect fuel and bring potable water, and some are in service too. They take part in social, ritual and religious activities. A pre-delivery ritual is celebrated in the seventh month of the first pregnancy and a post-birth ritual (*chhati*) is performed on the fourth or fifth day after childbirth. The tonsure (*mundan*) ceremony is performed for both boys and girls. A marriage is held at the bride's parent's house and a Brahman priest officiates over the rituals. Consummation of the marriage takes place at the bridegroom's residence. The Dhodia cremate the dead and the bones are disposed off in a river; the death ritual (*barwa*) is performed on the twelfth day.

The Dhodia depend on agriculture and agricultural labour; in addition to this they are also engaged in fishing. According to the census, 38.78 per cent of the Dhodia are returned as workers out of them, 50.93 per cent are cultivators, 21.41 per cent are agricultural labours, 12.89 per cent are in other-than-household industries and the remaining 14.77 per cent are engaged in other occupations. Every Dhodia clan has a chief known as the *agewan*. He is the spiritual and political head of the clan. The Dhodia have now established a registered association, the Samasta Dhodia Samaj, which works for the welfare of the community.

The Dhodia are Hindus and worship Mahadeo, Hanuman, Amba Mata, Kaka Balia, Bagh Devi etc. Kaneshari Devi, the deity of grains, is as Hindus, 0.07 per cent as Christians, and a small number as Jains, Muslims, Sikhs and Buddhists. The 1961 and 1971 census data do not show any significant change. They celebrate the festivals of Holi, Dhuleti, Mahashivaratri, Navratri, Krishna Janmashtami, Ganesh Chaturthi, Rakhi and Diwali. They sing folk-songs, dance the *garba* (a folk-dance from Gujarat) and play percussion instruments like the tur, drum etc. The Dhodia Community of Gujarat like the Chaudhri and Gamit were influenced by a number of Vaishnavite religious movements.

There are teachers, doctors, engineers and administrative officers among the Dhodias. Some of them have mastered the skill of tailoring and masonry work. They send their children to schools and colleges for higher education. This is evident from the census returns which show that they have attained a literacy rate of 44.96 per cent as compared to the general literacy rate of the scheduled tribes of the state (21.14 per cent). The male and female literacy rates are 56.38 per cent and 33.67 per cent, respectively. The Dhodia avail of facilities extended by the health care system, though they still continue to rely on their own medicine men.

The Dhodia inhabit the state of Maharashtra in areas adjacent to Gujarat, and the union territories of Dadra and Nagar Haveli, and Daman and Diu, where they are concentrated in the Talasari and Dahanu talukas of Thane. They number 10,980 individuals, out of which 56.69 per cent live in urban areas. The Dhodia of Maharashtra are bilingual; they speak Gujarati at home and also know the regional language Marathi. Their primary occupation is agriculture, but they also work as agricultural labourers, as labourers for the forest department and some are also employed in small scale industries.

In Dadra and Nagar Haveli, the Dhodia population is 13,796 (6799 males and 6997 females). The literacy rate here is 38.79 per cent (52.48 per cent males and 25.48 per cent females). Their surnames are Patel and Dhodi; they are divided into several exogamous clans like Banjaria, Bariya, Beigrahi, Attara, Bilarkhaw, Athi, Bamania, Mulgrahi and Parsi Mehta. In this union territory, the Dhodia are mainly engaged in cultivation besides toddy tapping, fishing, working as agricultural labourers, etc. The educated are employed in the government or in other organizations. They are in civil court staff of Silvassa Court. They worked with me when I was civil judge at Silvassa.

The Dhodia are also called Dhodi in Daman and Diu. According to the 1981 census their population is 1424. They speak Dhodi among themselves and with others either in Hindi or Gujarati. They are distributed in the villages of Kachigam, Dunetha, Damanwada, Zari, Patlara, Katheria, Moti Daman, Machhiwada and Magarwada of Daman. They are divided into nine exogamous clans (kul) namely Banjania, Baria, Parsi, Mehta, Bilarkhaw, Attara and others. They affix Dhodia and Patel to their names. They have a practice of giving *dahej* (bride price) and at present it is fixed atRs. 160. Divorce (*chutta-chedi*) is allowed in their society. Remarriage(*natra*) is allowed for the divorced and widowed of either sex. They conduct a ceremony on the fifth day (*pancho)* after birth as well as the naming and tonsure ceremonies.

They are mainly agriculturists. The Dhodia hold land as the tenants of the Koli Patel, Vania and Kamli Patel, and they pay an annual rent to their landlord. They have their own caste council for social control, namely the hamlet council (*faliya panch*) and village council (*nayat panch*). The Dhodia profess the tribal faith. The 1981 census returns 97.82 per cent of the Dhodia as followers of Hinduism and 2.18 per cent as Buddhists. They also worship Hindu deities. Their tutelary God is Lord Brahmadev. Their village deities are Samara Dev, Kakanwalia, Sitalamata, Petforio Mata, Mansari Mata etc. They believe in ghosts (*bhoot)* and to appease them, they offer food and liquor at every feast.

Katkari

Also known as Kathodi or Kathodia, they are concentrated in the Raigad and Thane districts of Maharashtra, where their settlements are along the foothills of the Sahayadri range. The Katkari are also distributed in Rajasthan, Gujarat, Dadra and Nagar Haveli. The Katkari are grouped with the Kathodi along with other subgroups in the order notifying them as a scheduled tribe in Maharashtra.

The Katkari are a short-statured, round-headed people. They have a broad nasal and facial profile. In the ABO blood group system, they exhibit a higher incidence of gene 'B' than gene 'A', and a very low proportion of non-secretors for ABH secretion in saliva. They show R1, predominantly a moderate frequency of R and the presence of the Rh type gene complex in the Rh blood group system. According to Mukherjee (1979), they exhibit a very low frequency of Hp1 allele. The incidence of sickle cell trait is comparatively low among them in comparison with other tribal groups of central and western India. G-6PD deficiency has been reported in a relatively moderate proportion in this group (7.8 per cent). The distribution of various other genetic markers reveals that they share similarities with the Proto-Australoid tribal groups of south and central India. Katkari are non- vegetarians who eat pork. Dry fish is eaten regularly by them. Rice, nagli and millet are their staple cereals. Alcoholic drinks, brewed at home and as well purchased from the weekly markets, are consumed. The Katkari females can be easily identified by their ornaments, especially ear-rings, tattoo marks on their forehead and arms and the style of wearing the saree above the knee.

The Katkari are divided into two endogamous divisions, namely the Son Katkari and the Dhor or Dhed Katkari. The Son Katkariare accorded a higher status. Each division is again divided into exogamous clans (devak) and phratries like Bahiri, Khanderao, Babadev, Bhawani and Parvati, and surnames like Pawar, Waghmare and Hilam (adnav). Enthoven (1922) mentioned some exogamous divisions among the Katkari. Although marriage by capture is permitted, negotiated marriages are the convention. Monogamy is the most popular form of marriage, though polygyny is allowed. Marrying the mother's brother's daughter and the father's sister's daughter is allowed. They pay a bride price and follow the patriarch rule of residence. The custom of child marriage has been replaced by adult marriage. A necklace, green glass bangles and a dot on the forehead are regarded as symbols of marriage. Divorce is permissible and a divorced person is allowed to remarry. The mixed extended type of family is common among them. The sons inherit ancestral property equally and the eldest son inherits the*mantle* of authority of his father. The women participate in agricultural activities and contribute to the family income by selling seasonal vegetables and jungle products at weekly markets. They take part in socio religious affairs and in the activities of the statutory village council (panchayat). However, they are not allowed to take part in the traditional community council. The name giving ceremony *(barsa)* is performed on the twelfth day after childbirth and tonsure (*mundan*) is observed in the sixth month. Marriage rituals are performed at the bride's natal house and a marriage feast is offered by the families of the bride and the groom. The marriage is consummated on the second night at the groom's residence. The dead are cremated and the ashes are immersed in a river. Death Pollution is observed for twelve days. The community council consists of five members and acts as a mitigating body for intercommunity disputes.

The traditional occupation of the Katkari was catechu-making. Now, their economy is based on agriculture. A number of them work as daily-wage labourers. Some of the Katkari are sharecroppers. Poultry farming has recently been introduced in the Katkari economy. It is also evident from the 1981 census returns that 16.09 per cent of their total workers (52.64 per cent of the total population) are returned under forestry, etc. which indicates their adherence to the traditional occupation of catechu-melding. This is followed by 59.50 per cent of the workers returned as agricultural labourers and only 11.34 per cent as cultivators. The remaining 13.07 per cent are returned from different occupational sectors. They do not accept food and water from the scheduled castes of the neighborhood. However, there is no such restriction for the neighboring tribals.

They believe in their traditional tribal religion, gods and associated goddesses. However, Hinduism has influenced their religious practices and life cycle rituals. The practice of sorcery is also common among them. They have religious specialists of their own and at the same time the services of the Brahman priest, the bhatjee are sought for worshipping Hindu gods and goddesses and for performing life cycle ceremonies. The 1981 census returns 99.32 per cent of the Kathodi, Katkari as followers of Hinduism, 0.16 per cent as Christians, 0.08 per cent as Muslims and 0.44 per cent as either following 'other religions' or as not having stated their religion. A small number of them are returned as Buddhists, Sikhs, Jains, etc. The 1961 and 1971 census shows the Hindu population to be 99.95 per cent and 99.85 per cent, respectively. The community has a rich oral tradition. Their dances are performed accompanied by folk-songs and percussion instruments. They participate in regional Hindu festivals with their Hindu neighbours.

Their response towards formal education has been poor. This is also endorsed by the 1981 census figures, which show that only 4.57 per cent of them are literate. The literacy level among the females is only 1.64 per cent, and 7.36 per cent of the males are literate. Immunization and other child welfare schemes have received a positive response from the community. They avail of the facilities provided under the public distribution system. Wood collected from the forest is their main fuel resource. They have their own medicine men that provide them with indigenous medical care. Of late, they have shown a favourable attitude towards modern medicine and sometimes visit health centers. They utilize electricity, drinking water facilities and postal services.

The Katkari are known as the Kathodi in Rajasthan and they have migrated to this part from Maharashtra. Their total population, including the Katkari and other subgroups, who have been notified together, is 2553 (1236 males and 1317 females) according to the 1981 census. Out of them, 97 per cent are returned from rural areas. They are mainly distributed in the Onga, Samicha, Parebati, Mubusha and Jbadol police station areas. They speak in their own dialect locally called Kathodi, which is a dialect of the Indo-Aryan language, Marathi. Some of them are conversant with Hindi. The Devanagari script is used for writing. Their staple food is roti made of wheat and maize. The existence of only two clans in the community, the Bokya and Dukre has been reported. A large section of them is engaged in forest labour. Some of them earn their livelihood by selling firewood and charcoal. Most of their households possess half an acre of land provided by the government. Some of them have availed of financial assistance from the government to undertake basketry as a means of livelihood.

In Gujarat, the Kathodi are distributed in the Surat, Bharuch, Sabarkantha and Dang districts. They speak a corrupt form of Marathi, an Indo-Aryan language, at home. Gujarati is used for inter-group communication. The Gujarati script is used by them. The Kathodi are divided into two groups, namely the Son Kathodi and the Dhor Kathodi, which are further divided into various clans like Vagher, Gangada, Chavda, Nayak, Mishal,

Kaver, Lakhan, Gavit, Savra, Pawar, Bhil, Dhum, Kokni, Deve, Mukanya etc. They are primarily agriculturists and agricultural labourers. A sizeable section of them work as forest labourers. They also collect and sell forest products like gum, honey, mahua etc. In the process of selling forest produce, they are linked with the Bohra and a few other communities. They have a cultivator-labour relation with the Koli, Garasia, Gamit etc.

In Dadra and Nagar Haveli, the Kathodi are distributed in the Amboliand Dapada panchayat areas with a population of only 74 persons (1981census). They are said to have been brought here by the Parsis during the Portuguese Rule. Kokni, an Indo-Aryan language, is spoken among them- selves and they use the Marathi language while conversing with others. The Devanagari script is used. There are a number of clans among them, namely the Bhoia, Wagh, Savera, Peghi and Panwar in Dadra and Nagar Haveli. The tanning of hide was their traditional occupation and they served as bonded labourers (karchi-chadeal) to the Parsis. They have now taken up agriculture in a big way. A few of them earn their living by manufacturing and selling charcoal. Some migrate to Gujarat seasonally in search of menial jobs.

The Kathedi profess Hinduism. A sacred specialist from the Kokna or Varli community conducts their life cycle rituals. According to the census of 1961, 1971 and 1981, all of them are Hindus. They are linked with the Parsis through a cultivator—labour relation. The community members are covered by different developmental programmes in the fields of health, education, employment generation and social forestry. However, the impact of formal education is yet to be felt among them. Only 3, out of 74 persons have been returned as literate, according to the 1981 census.

References:

The Kathodi, Katkari, etc. are also notified as a scheduled tribe in Karnataka and their population is 942 (1981 census). Ahir, Bagle, Baraph, Bhoj, Chavan, Dharkar, Diva, Gaikvaa Gangoda, Ghayare, Gotarna, Jam, Kamdi, Khutale, Maje, Misal, Mora, Mukane, Murkhute, Patkar, Pavar, Savad, Suvar, Vaghmare, Valid, Vardi, Vatase and Wagh.

Gurav, V.N., The Socio-Economic uplift the Scheduled Tribes in Maharashtra in his thesis of Ph.D, with Reference to the Katkari, Warlis and Koknas, (Bombay: University of Bombay, 1971unpublished).

Ishwad, C.S. and S.N. Naik, 'Population Genetics of Three Endogamous Groups of West India', 1984 (Cited by Bhatia & Rao, 1986).

Karve, I and V. Dandekar, Anthropometric, Measurements of Maharashtra; Deccan College Monograph Series No. 8 (Poona: Deccan College, Postgraduate and Research Institute, 1951).

Maharashtra Tribal Research & Training Institute, A Monograph of the Katkaris of Maharashtra State, Bombay.

Masavi, Mustali and G. Pandya, the Kathodis of Gujarat: A Socio-Economic Survey and a Development Plan (Ahmedabad: Tribal Research and Training Institute, Gujarat Vidyapith, 1987).

Mukherjee, B.N. 'Genetic Distance Analysis Among Nine Endogamous Population Groups of Maharashtra, India', Journal of Human Evolution, 8 (4), 1979.

Kokna

Also known as Kokni or Kukni or Kukna, they once inhabited Konkan the western coastal strip of Maharashtra. The Kokna are one of the principal tribes of Maharashtra. They are concentrated in the districts of Nasik, Thane and Dhule. The Kokna are bilingual. They speak Kokni, an Indo-Aryan language, at home and Marathi with others. The Devanagari script is used for writing. They are non-vegetarians but do not eat **beef**. Pork and goat meat are eaten occasionally. Rice is their staple cereal, supplemented with wheat and jawar or nagu. Groundnut oil is their cooking medium. Kokna men drink alcoholic beverages regularly, while women consume the same occasionally. The community is divided into exogamous clans (kul), namely Powar, Chauhan, Deshmukh, Dhom, Khanbat, Mahala, Rawat, Gaikewar, Thavil, Goali, Bhoya, Yadav, Tiwari, Thakra and Jopra. They use these clan names as surnames. They are generally a monogamous people, though polygyny is allowed in the community. The Kokna are permitted to marriage cross-cousins. Vermilion and anklets are the symbols of a married woman. Bride price, known as *pend* is very high among them and a good number of Kokna men, who are unable to pay it, remain unmarried. The family is normally nuclear. They are patriarch, and patrilineal people. The rule of inheritance follows the male line. The women participate in social, ritual and economic activities along with the men. They also work as daily-wage labourers or agricultural labourers and contribute towards the family income. At present they also take part in the activities of the statutory village panchayat. The community observes birth pollution for five days. Previously, marriage rituals were performed at the groom's house; nowadays marriages are solemnized at the bride's house. The Kokna cremate the dead. Their village council is headed by a ***mukhiya***. The traditional patil community council is headed by a regional Kokna council for the redress of their grievances. The Kokna profess the traditional form of religion. They worship their ancestors and Kansari (corn deity), Dongar (hill deity), Gaodeo (village deity) and Bhairao. Their priest (bhagat) is generally from their own community. The Kokna are primarily ploughing cultivators and wage labourers. A few members of the community hold salaried government jobs. The community has derived benefits from family planning programme, employment generation schemes and new innovations in the field of agriculture and child welfare schemes. However, they have shown little interest in banking facilities and continue to depend on private moneylenders.

In Gujarat, the major concentration of the Kokna is in the Valsad and Dang districts. In addition to their mother tongue, they are conversant with the Gujarati language and use the Gujarati script. Some of their clan names Mahla, Gaikwad, Raut, Thakaria, Baghri, Davir, Gavdi, Gavit, Jadavand Darvi. They are basically settled agriculturists, but now some have taken up various other occupations.

In Dadra and Nagar Haveli, the Kokna are distributed in sixty villages with a population of 13,770 (1981 census). These people use both Gujarati and Marathi for inter-group communication and the Devanagari script for writing, while their mother tongue remains Kokna. Here, they are divided into two endogamous subdivisions, the Kokna and the Christian Kokna. Some of their clan names are Bhoia, Mohia, Gavit, Chowdhry, Gavrhi, Gayakwad, Mahan, Kali, Gaveli, Chauhan, Ganghora, Thorat etc. They cremate the dead and erect a memorial stone. Slash and burn cultivation was their traditional occupation, while terrace cultivation is their primary occupation now. They propitiate deities like Hirwa Dev (clan deity) and Waghya (village deity). They avail of educational and health facilities.

The Kokna, Kokni, Kukna are also returned in small numbers from Karnataka (41 persons) and Rajasthan (165 persons) according to the 1981 census.

References

Ballal, K.D., Dapda: A Village in Dadra and NagarHaveli, Census of India, 1971, Series 1, Part vi-C (Delhi: Controller of Publications, 1974).

Enthoven, R.E., The Tribes and Castes of Bombay (Bombay: GovernmentCentral Press, 1922), vol. ii, PP. 265 - 6.

Gulati, R.K., 'Folklore and Population Control', Folklore, 25 (10), 1984, 185 - 96. Nag, N.G., Kokna: A Scheduled Tribe in Dadra and NagarHaveli (Ethnographic Note) (Delhi:Controller of Publications, 1980). Negi, R.S. and A. Maitra, ABO Blood Groups in Some Western andSouthern Indian Tribes, 1974 (unpublished)(cited by Majumdar and Roy, 1980).

Koli

With a population of 11.98 lakh, they are one of the largest notified tribal groups of the western part of India. They are spread over Gujarat, Maharashtra (the coastal areas through Thane and Colaba and over the ghats through Khandesh, Nasik, Ahmednagar to the southern and western fringes of Poona), Dadra and Nagar Haveli, Karnataka, and with a small population in Rajasthan and Orissa. The term Koli means a *fisherman.* This term, which is applied to a number of communities, only serves to cover a variety of occupations and different stages of socio-cultural development which are encountered among the various communities which make up this group. There is the Son Koli, who almost exclusively is fishermen, and, then there are the Vaitee Koli and the Mangela Koli. The Malhar Koli are 'water carriers' particularly in the arid(dry) regions. The Chunvalia Koli are agricultural labourers and the Talapada Koli are agriculturists. Enthoven (1922) stated that the Koli of Bombay, Deccan and Konkan were divided into three occupational groups, namely Dhor Koli, who are *bamboo cutters*; Mahadev Koli who are husbandmen, *cattle keepers* and labourers and Son Koli who are *fishermen*; while Hassan (1920) mentioned two endogamous tribes, namely Malhar Koli and Mahadev Koli. Thurston (1909) also reported that the Koli of South Kanara (in Karnataka) were fishermen and *boatmen*. Enthoven reported several divisions among the Koli. A segment of the Koli (Koli Rajputs) by reason of their control over resources rose to found petty kingdoms and became ruling lineages.

They are mostly of below medium stature, with a round head shape and a broad facial and nasal profile. The Koli of Gujarat shows a relatively high proportion of broader head shape and narrower noses than their counterparts in Maharashtra. On the whole, the Koli in their genetic makeup show distinctive features from the Gond and Bhil group of tribes.

According to legend, the Koli are the descendants of the black dwarf who is believed to have emerged from the body of the famous King Vena. In the Puranic story of Vena's death and its aftermath, the sages are said to have churned some parts of his body from which a darkish dwarf emerged. Commentators have been inclined to equate Nishada with the Koli. According to another tradition prevalent among the Mahadev and other Koli communities, *Valmiki, the author of the Ramayana,* is regarded as their ancestor. Their supposed connection with Valmiki rests on occupational identity. Valmiki's story as narrated in the Skanda Purana, describes him as the son of a Brahman brought up by a Kirata, and as the person who took to the ways of waylayers like the Kiratas. Owing to this aberrant activity, Valmiki was designated a Koli, or so it is said. The Koli are notified as a scheduled tribe only in the Kutch district of Gujarat.

Agri, Ahir, Band, Bhil, Bhiave, Bhirale, Chanchi, Dhor/Thkre, Helmar, Kabber, Karade, K/jar, Konkan, Kulparana, Mahadeu, Dongar/Raj, Malhar (also called Kunum, Chumli, Pann/Panbhari), Maratha, Marvi, Men— dale, MetalDhangar, Musaje/Bhandu, Nehre, Rahtadkar, Shingtoki, Son, Solesi (also called Kashti/ Lall-angoti), Swyavanshi, Tankri, Tayade, Thanka/ Christian and Wali.

References

Banker, M.P., 'Distribution of Sickle Cell Hemoglobin amongDifferent Tribal Groups inMaharashtra', Indian Journal of Hematology, 2 (4), 1984.

ChaterjeeB.K., 'Racial Components ofthe Tribal Populations of India, Presidentina1 Address', Proceedings of the Indian Science Congress, Fart II, 1955, pp. 146- 70.

Enthoven, R.E., The Tribes and Castes of Bombay (Bombay: Government Central Press, 1922), vol. II.

Griffiths, W.G., 'The Kol Tribe of Central India: Anthropometric Appendix VII, Journal of the Royal Asiatic Society of Bengal Monograph Series 2, 1946, pp. 312—15.

Hassan, S.S., The Castes and Tribes... The Nizam's Dominions, Hyderabad State (Bombay: Government Central Press, 1920).

Negi, R.S., 'Sickle Cell Trait Distribution in India', Ph.D. Thesis (Calcutta: Calcutta University, 1976) (unpublished).

Negi, R.S. and A. Mitra, 'ABO Blood Groups in Some Western and Southern Indian Tribes', 1974 (cited byMajumdar and Roy, 1982).

Koli, Chunvalia

Mostly distributed in the Surendra Nagar and Junagadh districts of Gujarat they are scattered in other parts of the state. They are said to have come from forty-four (chunvalis) villages situated somewhere in northern Gujarat and have been named so There is a view that they have descended from the Makwana tribe, whereas some maintain that they have descended from the Jhala Rajpur. They speak Gujarati, and use the Gujarati script. They are non-vegetarians but do not eat pork or beef. The staple cereals consumed by them are rice, wheat; bajra and jowar. In relation to other Koli groups such as the Talapada, Thakarda, Hedia etc., the Chunvalia Koli are accorded the lowest position. Their community is divided into a number of exogamous clans (ataks). Beth Raja talc is considered superior and the remaining ataks are equal. Each atak is a set of two names, like Degam-Chouhan, Gar-Chania, Degam-Makana etc. For the purpose of marriage, the second atak name is taken into consideration. A bride from one's mother's atak is not considered. The age marriage is nineteen to twenty-one years for boys and sixteen to eighteen years for girls. Polygyny is not allowed. Levirate and sororate are permitted. The Wearing of ivory bangles was compulsory for married women, but nowadays it is not so. Bride price is paid. The rule of residence is patrilineal. Ber tree

(*Zizipus-jujupa*) in their life cycle rituals is noticeable. They mainly subsist on agricultural labour both on a daily and an annual payment basis. They observe festivals like *Jiruti* and *Pola*. Family planning programmes have made a significant impact on them. Some of them have benefited from the rural employment generation programs.

References

Bhattacharya, S., 'Field Notes on Nahali', Indian Linguistics, 17, 1957, pp. 245—58. Census of India, Special Tables on Scheduled Castes and Scheduled Tribes, Census of India, 1971, Part IV - A (Delhi: Controller of Publications, 1975).

Enthoven, R.E., The Tribes and Castes of Bombay (Bombay: Government Central Press, 1920; rpt. 1975, Delhi: Cosmo Publications), vol. I, pp. 174 - 5.

Russell, R.V. and Hiralal, The Tribes and cities of the Central Provinces of India (London: Macmillan and Company, 1916; rpt. 1975, Delhi: Cosmo Publications), vol. IV, p. 257.

Naikda / Nayaka

Each of their two divisions consists of a few exogamous clans (kul). But, Enthoven (1922) reported a few surnames among the Naikdas, namely Damara, Tadwala, Anosa, Bamna, Ujwala, Andharia, Rarhwa and Dhanka. Some urban Nayaka use the term *'Patel'* along with their names to elevate their social position. They are monogamous and usually seek alliances through negotiation. Bride price is paid in their marriage. They are patrilineal. The women use anklets, ear-rings and vermilion as the symbols of marriage. Divorce is permitted among them with the consent of the community council. A widow can remarry her deceased husband's younger brother after six to twelve months. Nuclear as well as vertically extended types of families are most prevalent among them. Sons inherit the father's property, but a woman can inherit the property if she has no brother. Women take part in social, economic, religious activities, and play a significant role in rituals. Certainrites are performed for a newborn baby on the fifth or sixth day after birth purificatory rites arc observed on the eleventh day. Marriage rituals continue for three days. The dead are usually buried and mourning is observed for three days. The purificatory rite is performed on the ninth or tenth day.

The primary occupations of the Nayaka are cultivation and agricultural labour. They are also engaged as carpenters while some are employed in timber industries. The Nayaka children also work as wage labourers. The Nayaka have community councils at certain places, which settle their social disputes. At other places, such councils have been replaced by statutory bodies. The Nayaka are Hindus and worship Brahmadev as their chief God. Many Gods of the wider Hindu pantheon are also worshipped. They celebrate the festivals of Holi, Deepavali, Dussehra, Divasa and perform death rites on Shivaratri day. Brahman priests conduct their marriage rites, while death rites are presided over by the Nayaka priest, Bhuva. Until recently, they used to act as sacred specialists during the marriage rituals the Dhodia. A few of them have been influenced by the preaching's of Jalaram of Virar and some Muslim saints. The community has a heritage of folk-songs. The women sing during marriages. As agriculturists and labourers, they have socio-economic relations with the neighboring communities. Public places including sources of water are shared with them. A few members are employed as teachers. They have their indigenous methods of family planning, but also avail of modern methods. The facilities of drinking water through dug-wells, pipelines and hand-pumps are provided. Electricity, road and rail transport are available to them.

Mass media, communication, economic assistance from government agencies; child welfare programmes, public distribution system and banking facilities are being availed of to a considerable extent by them. The Naikda are concentrated in the Dahanu and Palghar talukas of Thane district. They speak Katkari, a dialect of Marathi, for both intra- and inter-group communication. The Devanagari script is used by these people. The Naikda are divided into several exogamous clans, some of which are Pawar, Lahange, Ardi, Aide, Wagh, Pardhi, Saura, Bhandanga, and Phasale. These are also used as surnames. Marriage, to one's mother's brother's daughter and father's sister's daughter is permitted. The women take part in agricultural operations and sometimes work as wage labourers. Some children of this community also work as wage earners. Previously, the Naikda of Maharashtra used to collect the hide of dead animals, which some of them does even today. Agriculture is the major occupation of the community at present. Besides, they are engaged as wood cutters and labourers. The women are sometimes employed in collecting edibles, fodder, fuel, medicinal roots and barks from the forest, plucking flowers and berries.

They also collect leaves for beedi-making. The Naikda are Hindu by religion, and worship deities like Narayan, Bhawani, Kalika, Mahalakshmi. They respect the tiger (baghdra), which is regarded as a village deity and worshipped before solemnizing any marriage. Their own medicine man (*bhagat*) performs certain rituals. The festivals of Diwali and Holi are observed, and they attend the annual fair in connection with the worship of the Goddess Mahalakshmi. The Naikda women are skilled in wall painting and drawing with rice powder. The Naikda folk-songs are sung by both men and women to the accompaniment of their traditional musical instruments like the flute and the drum. They continue to depend on traditional medicines and are reluctant to visit hospitals. These hospitals, however, are located away from their settlements.

Varli

They inhabit the states of Maharashtra and Gujarat, and the union territory of Dadra and Nagar Haveli. The term Varli has been derived from the word *varal,* meaning uplanders. Enthoven (1922) observed that the Varli were semi-nomadic and lived in small groups under their own headmen. The Varli of Maharashtra are distributed in the districts of Greater Bombay, Raigadh, Nasik, Dhulia, Jalgaon, Ahmednagar and Poona. Their largest concentration, however, is in the Dahanu taluka of Thane district. The Varli are generally of below medium height, with a round head shape, broad face and more often short and broad nose (Karve and Dandekar, 1951).). They are non-vegetarians but avoid beef and pork. Their staple food is rice, supplemented with jawar and wheat. Milk consumption is negligible. They are fond of alcoholic drinks prepared from molasses and of the kind available at local shops as well. The Varli have four endogamous divisions, Suddha or pure Varli, Murde, Davar and Nihir. There are more than forty exogamous social divisions (kul) among them, based on surnames. Enthoven (1922) noted some of their exogamous kuls like Bantria, Bhangara, Bhavar, Bhendar, Gambhale, Jadhar, Jadhare, Karbat, Kirkire, Kondaria, Meria, Miske, Nikhade, Nimbore, Pagi, Pileyana, Ravatia and Sarkar. Mates are generally acquired either through negotiation or by rendering service. The Varli practices polygyny occasionally. The first marriage is called **lagan** and the second and subsequent marriages are called **nowli**. Neddaces and toe-rings are the symbols of marriage for women. Residence after marriage is patrilineal. Bride price, *des*, is paid both in cash and kind. Divorces take place mostly due to adultery, mental derangement and sterility. In a post-divorce situation, the father becomes the custodian of the children. A divorced person may remarry. Age at marriage is twelve to sixteen years for girls and seventeen to twenty years for boys. Their families are mostly vertically extended. The father's property is equally inherited by all sons, and authority passes down from the father to the eldest son. The women take part in economic activities. Among the Varli, birth pollution lasts for thirty days. The childhood rituals observed by them are those connected with naming and tonsure of the child. The marriage is solemnized at the bride's natal house. The dead are cremated, but infants are buried. There is a council of Varli elders, which settles disputes within the community. In case the dispute remains unsettled, the police patil, who is a Varli, settles the dispute.

The cases of intercommunity disputes are solved by the sarpanch of the statutory panchayat. The traditional council at the hamlet level is headed by the *Kabhari* and at the village level by the *Patil*. Their village deities are Gamdevi and Vaghdeo. Their major festival is Shun. The role of the sacred specialist in this community is negligible. There is a medicine man called Bhagat. Most of the Varli houses display graphics on the walls drawn with rice powder. They also make mats from date leaves. Both the men and women among the Varli are painters. The women paint in white with touches of brilliant gerua (saffron) red on the walls of their homes which are earthy brown in colour. These pictographs are made to celebrate festivals. They are fond of music and dance and have traditional folk-songs and folk-tales. The primary and traditional occupation of the Varli is agriculture. The subsidiary occupation is wage labour in agriculture and on fruit orchards owned by the Parsis. The Varli exchange labour amongst themselves. For medical help, they first consult the Bhagat. In case he fails, they visit hospitals. The attitude of these people to family planning programmes is positive. The public distribution system functions in their area through fair-price shops. The Varli of Gujarat are mostly settled in the mountainous districts of Dangs and Valsad. They are divided into three groups, namely Davar, Murde and Nehri. Among themselves, they speak the Varli language, but they are also conversant with Gujarati and use the Gujarati script. Some of their clans are totemic, but others are similar to the Maratha Rajput clans.

The Varli are a landholding community in Gujarat, but practice a primitive form of agriculture. Wage labour, fishing and the collection of forest produce are other occupations. The Varli are also returned from Karnataka and Goa, Daman and Diu, and their population figures are 700 and 800, respectively (1981 census).

References:

Dalmia, Yashodhara, The Painted World of the Warli: Art and Ritual of the Warli Tribes of Maharashtra (New Delhi: LalitKalaAkademi, 1988).

Enthoven, RE., The Tribes and Castes of Bombay (Bombay: Government Central Press, 1922; rpt. 1975, Delhi: Cosmo Publications), vol. 111, 445-55.

Jayakar, Pupul, The Earth Mother (New Delhi: Penguin Books, 1989).

Karve, and V.M. Dandekar, Anthropometric Measurements of Maharashtra, Deccan College Monograph, Series No. 8 (Poona: Deccan College, Postgraduate and Research Institute, 1951).

Maihotra, R. and S.K. Mandal, 'Warlis of Gujrat', in TribesinContemporary India (Calcutta: Anthropological Survey of India, 1984) (unpublished).

Mandal, S.K. and R Maihotra, 'Warli of Gujarat: A Profile', Tribe (Udaipur), 15 (1 & 2), 1983, pp. 27—40.

Mashe, Juiya Soma, The Warlis: Tribal Paintings and Legends (Bombay: Chamould Publications and Arts, 1982).

Negi, R.S., Sickle Cell Trait Distribution in India, Ph.D. Thesis (Calcutta: Calcutta University, 1976) (unpublished).

Negi, R.S. and A. Maitra, 'ABO Blood Groups in Some Western and Southern Indian Tribes', 1974 (Cited in Majumdar and Roy, 1982).

Pandya, Gaurish, 'Dungri Warlis', Adivasi (Ahmedabad), 4 (1), 1981, pp. 104-89. Parulekar, Godavari, Adivasi Revolt: The Story of Warli Peasants in Struggle (Calcutta: National Book Agency, 1975).

(Save, K.) The Warli (Bombay: Padma Publications, 1945).

Singh, K.S., Tribal Society in India: An Anthropo-historical Perspective (Delhi: Manohar Publications, 1985).

Position of Woman in Santhal Society

Women are the part and parcel of every society. They are the base stone of every family and every society. Moreover, it is proved from innumerable studies that women are the object of utmost victimization in any point of transition (Sahu, 1996). In Santhal society after marriage bride and bridegroom become life partner and they find new relations. There is no word in Santhal like husband or lord for man and wife for woman. Husband calls his wife as *Begait* and wife also calls her husband as *Bagait*. Hence Begait is a common word which indicates that there is no domination of husband over wife. The relation of a Santhal wife and husband is romantic by nature. If a wife is fairly good and hard working then the husband though feels proud of it but remains anxious too that she may leave him. So along with love and respect a sense of doubt always hunts him, he keeps watch on her movements. Sometimes husband expresses his doubt and fear and tries to get promise from her wife not to leave him. Of course, there is no hard and fast rule of domination of husband over wife but the husband being elder and stronger applies physical strength. A wife cannot stop her husband. Due to impact of Hindu society a tendency is growing among the Santhal males to establish them as superior forcibly by using several proverbs. Women's position is also going to decrease due to so many factors. The widows have been getting more victimization in the present situation. A wife is considered a great importance in a man's life. A man having no wife is looked down and has less importance in the society. Brahmcharya has no importance and is unbelievable.

A Santhal wife and husband cannot call the name of each other. A woman cannot be called by her name in her in-laws. It is great interesting and funny too that even mother-in-law does not know the name of her daughter-in-law. A child of 12 years does not know his/her mother's name. As soon as conception is recognized a Kandu is consulted and roots, few mustard seeds, a piece of iron are put to her neck. The pregnant woman has to obey certain taboos. An old woman takes care of pregnant woman. A woman is respected by the Santhals. A woman confirms right over the family after having a child. A childless woman lives in insecurity. A woman having many children is compared with crabs, which is no doubt insulting but having only girls are insulting and compared with pigs or bitches. In Santhal society is not too much dependent on husband so she can leave him if she is harassed. So man is also anxious about his wife whether she may propose to leave him any time. The mother has a little role in taking decision in negotiation of marriage, but she is being informed all the matters duly. A girl does not have any power to take decision or choice, except if she is extremely rigid. In negotiation and Koda Dhoti no women except groom's mother takes part publically. In

Madoa or any other sacred work woman has no role she has to be order only. It is mother who for the last time feeds the son in presence of ancestral spirits at Manjhitban and gives permission to marry. All rituals related to marriage are performed by women except carrying the bridegroom on basket at the time of vermillion.

In the changing social situation women are losing their social, economic degradation and women's freedom. Santhal society are also having all these privileges but loosing so many privileges. Economic insecurity among the widow is very much haunting problem. The social problem is more among aged women than men. However, their proportion uniformly declined from 1961 to the 1981 periods. The main reason why widows out-number widowers may be because men used to be older than women by 5 years or more years at the time of their marriage. In addition, they are exposed to greater environmental risk than women. The plight of widowhood is severe and discriminatory among women and consequents they suffer more than widowers. Generally men remarry after the death of their wives, but widows do not have similar social sanction. Of course, the Santhal widows have socially sanctioned to have remarriage but it is depend upon the situation and age of the widows. This indicates inequality between men and women and low status of the women. In addition, widows face many other handicaps in daily lives, being forbidden from wearing clothes of their choice and from attending auspicious functions. Therefore, widowhood is a curse for the aged in the Santhal society. Hence, urgent legal and social changes may be brought about to reduce the discrimination shown against the widows in Santhal society. In so many cases the people are casting them aside as useless keep them alone and neglect. They feel aloof, frustrated and discarded. This is not equal among all the families. Among the poorer, they have still their importance and craze for the aged widows. They keep them with love and get love and affection also. There is a burning problem how this society will handle this problem in the future. It is an open question because they are in a period of transition or in a tribe-caste continuum.

Women of ability have appeared in every age and in every society, but cultural definitions based on gender have shaped women's behaviour and placed them in the roles that feature passivity, subordination, detachment and even social parasitism. In a number of respects, females have an advantage over males. They matured somewhat faster, due to specific circumstance which may well account for the consistently greater productivity of girls in achievement of skills. Females show much lower visible incidence of number of deleterious genetic traits such as baldness, colour blindness and hemophilia. The reason is that the X chromosome contains many more genes than the Y one, which is among the males. Chromosomal composition may help to explain the greater longevity and resistance to some diseases that female show. They have lower mortality rate in all age groups. The girls reach sexual maturity earlier than boys with much individual variation, usually six months earlier than their mothers. And they come to the stage of old age in the same way.

But before reaching to the old age men and women having variations enjoy biological satisfaction of food and sex, logical from the games, telling stories and riddles, music, singing, beating drums etc. in marry making, wandering in the ingles hills and on the banks of the rivers engaging themselves in, hunting and collection roots and shoots. They pass stages of socialization like adolescence and adulthood and family life and attending old age. They try to maintain and perception about their culture and creed. Total number of widows has been classified in to four broad classes. As we know that the Santhals economic condition is very poor few families are in a position to afford both meals for all family members. On the basis of their food consumption they have been categorized as two meals for 6 months, two meals for 3 months, one meal for the year and one meal for 6 months and less. The highest percentage (47.7%) of widows belongs to the families who are having only one meal for the whole year and the lowest (4.5%) belongs to those families who are in a position to afford two meals for six months. The widows of the families with both meals for 3 months occupy third position (36.5%).

Widowhood

Problems of the widows vary from society to society. The widows are subjected to many restrictions and are reflected in their action, pattern and ways of life. In this situation, it can be said that the 'caste' has also a distinctive role. The higher the caste, the greater the restriction and lower the caste, the less restrictions. All these can be seen in their day to day life. But in Santhal society the widows have comparatively less restrictions. Their important aspects of restrictions are to be seen in wearing dress, in taking of food, performance etc. In Hindu society the widows are strictly prohibited from coloured apparel or Sari or red bordered cloth which are used by the married women. Atypical piece of cloth totally known as *'than'* is prescribed. In a few cases black border with small stripe Saris are used by widows. There is no hard and fast rule for wearing certain prescribed dress for Santhal widow, even than they generally wear the cloth. Use of ornament of different types is very common among the Hindu society especially among the Bengali women. The love of using ornament has been seen among the highly educated sophisticated ladies. The women belonging to well to do families use gold ornaments while silver or other metallic ornaments are being used by the women of less fortunate people. The Santhal are very- poor so they cannot afford to bear the cost of gold ornaments. On the occasion of marriage they use some kinds of silver or other metallic ornaments. After the death of the husbands the widows generally not use ornaments but there are no strict rules except few items. In some cases, it is found that they use different printed saris with some ornaments. In Hindu society, sudden drop of food items is an important factor of restriction among the widows. After becoming widows they are not allowed to non-vegetarian diet especially among the higher castes, but such type of restriction has been seen among the widows of lower caste. It is up to the widow which diet she will adopt. In Santhal society too no restriction of taking diet has been seen. On asking the, widows inform that we never think anything about to have or not to have the kinds of dishes. They enjoy almost all dishes which are common for general people. In some of the Hindu societies the widows have to receive their food in certain plates. For instance, orthodox Brahmin widows prefer *stone plates* indicating their austere life-style. But it is a costly affair and these are breakable too. Naturally, a bell metal plate or a glass plate is used for this purpose. But in Santhal society there is no question of bell metal or glass plate. They use only aluminum utensils as their economic condition does not allow them to purchase brass utensils or other costly ones except in few families. There is no separate plate for the widow; of course 4 or 5 aged widows have been seen with separate plates and lotas. This does not mean that they have any different view for the widows. In some of the Hindu families in respect of cooking, using the common crockery during cooking there are some restriction which are to be meticulously maintained by some widows. Affluent widows have separate kitchen as well as separate utensils for this purpose. In some cases the widows adhere to observe some days, i.e. Bear and Barat like Ekadashi when fasting restricted food taking is done by them. These ritual formalities are believed to earn merit in the next life and at the sometime it is considered expiration for the misdeed she has done in the present term of her life time. Naturally, these are imposed by traditions and customs and are followed in many ways without be grudging. But the Santhal is a pure naturalist. They do not have imaginational life.

They celebrate Sarhul, Karma, Sohrai etc. in which all members take part with full joy. There is no difference between non-widows and widows. The widows enjoy these festivals as good as equally. In Hindu society hair shaving and tonsuring is by many widows. These are the formalities maintained by some, because as a part of austere life they would like to lose their feminine beauty by which they may look attractive and are lured to do misdeed in the form of sex offences. Hence, some widows shave their hair, gradually fading away their gloss, beauty and charm. At the sometime, some widows take initiation from a preceptor (Guru) through regularly uttering God's name and sometimes using a typical bead necklace or string of beads of rosary or the stem of sacred basil plant. Widows sit and offer prayer to God with a murmuring sound of chanting. But in the case of Santhal this type of work is heinous and unbearable. Regarding maintaining the feminine beauty they use natural leaves and flowers.

In case a woman becomes widow in the early age then she is allowed to choose her life partner again. But for those who become widows after 40 years then this is the crucial period for them. In this age they are having so many children and it is not an easy task to leave all the children in their parental house and have another life partner. They remain busy with their domestic work to fulfill their basic needs. They do not find any leisure to remain engage in any religious talk. So the Santhal widows have wider prosperity in comparison to other society.

It is a fact that Hindu widows have a special stigma and curse and sometimes the aging and insolvent widows have to encounter many problems of varied nature than the Santhal Community. It is to be remembered that Hindu widows have to bear the work tradition under which they have grown. They have to feel that they are unhappy as their husbands pre-deceased them and this they think is due to their sin committed by them either in this life of in the earlier life. This guilty conscience has made them a subject of 'exterior' individuals in a family and they have no other alternative than to think themselves as dishes fit for God alone or inhabitants of the other world. Many more affluent widows have to stay permanently in some sacred and holy place, like Kasi, Brindavan, Mathura, Haridwar with this bent of mind, where many sacred centers in the form of temples or shrines are in existence. There they have to live an austere life, worship gods, listen to devotional songs, religious discourses and many other things dilated to spiritual life, just for their salvation. They were great religions leaders in the past who preached a life for salvation after death and their doctrines are now followed by these widows in letter and spirit. In this way we can very well-understand the real picture of Hindu society but the materialistic and imaginary people of India have not come into the point to explain the falseness and unbelievable deeds of the concerned society. The Santhal and other tribal people of India have rightly marked the in heinous deeds of the Aryans in the very beginning when they were penetrating India.

In the Santhal society there is no any religious center to accommodate the Santhal widows for washing the Gods and preaching the speech of sacred Guru. The aged widows become the care taker, teacher and well wisher of the young boys and girls who join the **Giti Ora** (youth dormitory). In some places there is only one Giti Ora common both boys and girls whereas in some other places separate Giti Oras boys and girls have been seen. The dormitory is known as an educational center as well as an institution of sex. It is a house for bachelors normally situated in a prominent part of the village. It is, in fact, a school for social training where a boy of 11centers to learn way of life and leaves only when he is a useful member of the community. Although lot of changes has killed the age old traditions, there are certain villages which have been maintaining such houses with a great difficulty and opposition too. In December every year, arrange a feast where the elders of the village are invited. They exchange greeting and dance with the members. In the past, the main function of these dormitories was to train village youth in singing and dancing. They used to dance in front the dormitory every night. The dormitory for the girls was not a public place were anybody could go. It was in a secret building where girls used to sleep at night. An old woman/widow used to supervise the function of the dormitory. Any one active girl among the members was selected as monitor of the house. She used to control the dormitory in the absence of the leady supervisor.

In a recent survey it has been found that dormitory has totally disappeared in most of the villages in the real form where they have adopted modernity i.e. Hinduism. Nowadays there is a change in costume and living. But these changes have not changed the form structure of the Santhal life. They are the most serious people take pride in their traditional life and culture. They are very particular about their dialect and are proud of their language, their habit, their life and culture. The on-rush of the waves of culture contact has not deterred them from their true trait and traditions for ages and they are sure to maintain their ethos and world view intact in future. Hence, the problem of sending the widows to certain places will not enter into the Santhal society. Thus, we see that the aged widows are facing many acute problem of which the four-health, physical, economic and socio-psychological are very important. Problem of health is very important to the aged widows. During the old age, power of resisting a disease diminishes. They become ill due to the frequent attach of various diseases and no medicine can cure them completely. In the case of Santhal aged widows only 42.4 per cent are getting adequate treatment. 57.6 per cent are not getting proper medicine and care due to their poor socio-economic condition and few other reasons. They are mostly suffering from rheumatic, gastric, liver trouble etc. in which half of them are usually disable. The Santhal being the herbal doctor believe in indigenous treatment including *Jharphunk.* 76.0 per cent widow's diseases are cured by their tradition treatment whereas only 6.0 per cent referring belief on medicinal treatment. In worst case they take the patients to the hospital. 53.4 per cent widows are showing moderate health status while 56.8 per cent widow's present mode of life is good. Due to old age, different age related changes are found among the Santhal widows' physiology. Regarding vision problem majority of the age widows have no such problem. Few of them are the victims of diminishing visual acuity. About 50 per cent of the aged widows are suffering from cataract but very few have undergone eye operation. Those who have lost more than half of their teeth are facing gastro-intestinal problem. Few Santhal widows are suffering from other physical problems such as hearing problem, skeletal problem, breathing problem, nervous system problem, skin problem, kidney problem etc., but they are not getting proper treatment and care due to their poor socio-economic condition. The most common difficulty among them is poor eye-sight and impaired hearing capacity. Thus, the aged widows suffer from one or more physical problems but majority of them are capable to undertake certain personal tasks without the assistance of others. During the illness the family members provide help and co-operate them at any time. They get more help from their daughters. Old age is characterized by economic insecurity, ill health, loneliness, resistance to change and failing mental and physical power. They become weak even than they remain busy in domestic works. The widows have to face economic problems either due to their insufficient income or no income at all. During economic crisis they are not in a position to fulfill their needs and desire. This automatically creates so many socio-psychological problems among them. It has been found that the Santhal widows have some socio psychological problems. Very few widows have reported that they are getting almost all support from their family members so they do not live under pressure where are majority of them are not happy with the fully support from their families. They keep themselves busy in household work more than male even than they feel more isolated than the males. They also complain that they no more get the same kind of treatments from their family members as they used to get during their young age. Some of them feel themselves as social burden for their respective families.

The Santhal Aged Widows

Women in general are attributed as second sex even in global society. They as a part and parcel of the community could not remain passive in social transition. It is proved from innumerable studies that women are object of utmost victimization in any point of transition. No one society can demand any achievement without acceptance of women's share in it. Women are in fact, the base stone of every family and every society. They too, therefore accept the toils of a transition or change. Indian modern literature depicts a few records on the Santhal women so far. But history has made a Santhal woman as strong laborious being only. Their contribution to the history is never identified. So many mothers and wives have scarified their sons and husbands for the sake of the existence and identity of the race.

The aged women and aged widows are of special contribution. The status of women in Santhal society is very clear. It holds the view that woman is, at least, as vital to life and society as man. This society has given so many privileges to the women such as the rights, privilege and freeness, more in comparison to the Aryan society. The woman is acknowledged as an independent personality in possession of human qualities and receiving rewards for her deeds. In Santhal society there are few restrictions on the part of women, but at the same time it is admitted that constructive participation of the women is necessary for development of the family. The Santhal widows have almost the same sole for the smooth running of the family and development of the family but unfortunately the widows of the area under study were kept in isolation. They used to suffer from various social disabilities. They were not allowed to express their opinion in family matters and other social affairs.

Widowhood is a typical life situation. Concise Oxford Dictionary defines a widow as, a woman who has lost her husband by death and has not married again (1982). As it happens, she has to live with other members of her family and sometimes alone indicating a distinct social position. It is true that different cultures and societies have prescribed distractive rules of conduct signifying very clearly her status, role and privileges in a particular society. India is a typical caste-ridden society, but the autochthones tribal groups are the early settlers. The tribes as we know are those people who had been historically known as different from the Aryan people and since very prehistoric period they have been known as non Aryans. Not only in India but globe wide in so many other countries tribal people are found and among them the kith and kins of Santhal too are present who are named somewhat in different ways but a socio scientific study reveals the fact that their rituals, their customs and ways of living in many ways constitute the very norms of tribal identity.

After arrival of the Aryans we find series of convergence of other groups and through these historical processes of assimilation and blending, re-structured the whole Indian society giving some distinguishable and identifiable characters. Naturally, the condition of the widows varies from society to society indicating their distinctive position role and status as prescribed in those particular societies. Some societies allow remarriage of the widows whereas in others it is not allowed. The situation of widowhood in Hindu social system is of some different nature. It denies many more facilities and happiness and compels them to accept a style of life which is completely different from the earlier one. Widowhood brings many changes to the status and roles of the affected women. The status and roles mostly based upon the age of a widow. Widowhood at the prime youth of a woman is considered to be a curse. It has reflections on her, as if she is the cause of her husband's death and thereby she may be treated as a sinner and inauspicious personality. In her family, her position or fate is certainty in dilemma and sometime derogatory (Manna & Chakravarty, 1991).

Thus, widows of different age-groups of different castes and economic status pursuing different ways of earning exist. All these things and many more deep-rooted prejudices and cultural obligations have created a situation which apparently appear to be more problematic. Social injustices, less cohesion in the social organization have practically exposed the problems in different ways in the tribal societies; the Santhal too there is a wider scope and facilities for the widows. But the wave of Aryan culture has been encroaching upon the tribal society. And now the tribal widows are facing so many problems. Under such a condition, the anthropologist, psychologist, gerontologist and social workers should take note of these things and try to diagnose the problems in their true picture and perspective, and suggest remedial measures. If we have a look over the position of the widows in the labyrinthine and bye lanes of the historical processes, then we can visualize the situation in different light. Ancient society in the remotest past cherished a promiscuous social stage, later supreme posed on her by the rule of the dominant male. This obstreperous state of affairs has been described by many as gerontocracy. Later on, changes in economic viability due to climatic influences and gradual spread of knowledge by harnessing the nature, a different relationship began to emerge demanding a new role of the individuals in different societies. Through some historical factors of interaction, assimilation and composition this appeared in the societies, and in India, we have certain records of the some through traditions, and in later period, by religious doctrines which have been handed down to the posterity.

Many believe that Hinduism is a flexible religion which assimilated and buttressed many more situations and thus, with its wide spectrum, it appeared very distinctively unlike other prevalent puritan faiths. During the Vedic period, we have had records in which the so-called pastoral semi nomadic Aryan group of people had the advantage of composing the Veda. The earliest Veda is the Rig-Veda which was recited approximating in 1000 B.C. and the other Vedic age is considered to have been prolonged and fused slowly up to 600 B.C. This is considered 600 B.C. to 200 B.C. and gradually it lost, merged in to the Epic age (500 B.C. to 400 A.D.). Thereafter, many more dominating doctrines reflected through Dharmshastras and Sunnite considered prevailing up to 500 A.D. Many other new religious doctrines in the form of Jainism, Buddhism etc. appeared and all these together titled the core pattern of the life, outlook and life style. Many scholars tried to evaluate the status of women and these have been published by Tarafdar (1936), Altekar (1938), Indra (1940), Shastri (1952), Kapadia (1955), Jayal (1960), Paul (1961), Sengupta (1970) and Manna and Chankravorty (1991). But many are of opinion that even in the darkest days of year the position of the widows in the Hindu society was not as deplorable as it happened in the later period, which have rhythm reflections even to-day, as Indra (1940) has asserted: 'During Vedic period marriage as Union between a man and a woman before the nuptial fire, and was held to be the most unbreakable and subsisting even after death. Though monogamy was undoubtedly a prevalent custom, polygamy in the form of polygamy or polyandry also in vogue. Child marriage, in ancient times, among the Hindus, was not considered justifiable and as a result, there was no question of child widows. Even in Hindu tradition, there was a custom of levirate (marriage between the widow of the deceased elder brother), which has been very rightly described as '***Niyoga***' of course, the Athrva Veda XVIII: 2, 1 described it as:

It was customary for the widow to lie by the side of her husband's corpse on the funeral pyre, she was, however, asked to

come down and a prayer was offered that
she should lead a prosperous life enjoying the
bliss of children and wealth (Altekar, 1938).

None-the-less, Indra (1940) emphasized that after
300 B.C. the widows' position began to deteriorate. A
great controversy arose over the Niyoga custom. It is
undesirable that customs like child marriage polygamy
were rarely appearing on the social scene without
disturbing the normal healthy life of widows. In the period
of Dharmsastra, a hard life of renunciation was prescribed
for natural widows leading to austerity as asserted by
the law-givers, i.e. Manu Janyavalka, Vishnu Sharma etc.
The concept of **Patibrata** was sanctioned and gradually
popularized by then. The prime duty of a faithful wife
was to give unstinted services to the husband. It was
reiterated that death of the husband could not break their
tie of unity, i.e. undivided, eternal relation Manu, the
ancient law giver, recommended and prescribed that: "A
wife should lead the life like the shadow of her husband
by sacrificing many things. She should not take meal in
two times, she should take only fruits during Ekadasi (i.e.
eleventh day of the moon, both in brighter and darker
halves) on full moon days, she should never utter the
name of any man who is considered 'Parapurush' or a
paramour. A woman becomes a widow owing to her evil
activities or unchaste life of her earlier birth, She should
therefore, be mindful of her responsibilities and should
strictly perform the religions duties in order to get rid of
evil effect of the sins she committed (Sengupta, 1970).

With this the rigorous belief, a peculiar **Sati** custom began to become popular i.e. on the funeral pyre of the husband, the widow was sacrificed forcibly with a deafening cries and the sound of beating of drum under which her lamentation and groaning would down. This custom became wide spread and the Hindus belonging to higher caste adhered to it. Later, Raja Ram Mohan Roy, a famous social reformer took this up with the then ruling British Government and got a low enacted by which 'Sati' custom became a sinful act and punishable. Of course in Vishnu Sambita, Sati was recommended). Pandit Iswar Chandra Vidyasagar (1881), another scholar and social reformer, tried to introduce widow remarriage by searching its sanctions from many Sanskritic scriptures. Thus, it is found that after 600 A.D. **Niyoga** marriage went out of fashion, because the concept of **Patibrata**, i.e. devotion of wife to husband got prominence. Child marriage became popular due to Muslim penetration in the country. The marriage at the age of 8 years - the Gouidban - indicating a means of earning merit and salvation. Regarding Sati, it is not recorded whether the widows preferred to have voluntary death lying on the pyre of the deceased husband due to unforeseen austere and painful life ahead. In Indian soil, widows have many problems belonging to any age. But when the adjective "aged" is used, the widows are grouped in a small compartment with its own problems. A woman, who is a widowed, is considered as an unfortunate, an unlucky or an ill-fated person. A guilty mind looms large on them with a belief that possibly this particular woman perhaps did a great sin in her past life and in consequence she has lost her husband and as if she herself is responsible for the short life of her spouse. The society projects and blames her in this way and ultimately, this sense of supposed guilt is ingrained in her mind and accordingly she feels herself an out caste in the society. Coming to the Indian tribal context, a different outlook has been seen. The Indian tribes-called aboriginal or autochthones because of their being the earliest inhabitants of this country, not only belong different stages of culture but they vary from area to area in regard to size of the population, language, racial types, socio-economic organisation etc. They have always been exploited by the clever and economically powerful groups. The tribal problem is much more complex than the rural-urban problem. A few generations ago, the tribal life was well adjusted. Today, there is neither adjustment nor happiness in the life-pattern. Their culture soil has been constantly eroded by the dangerous floods of Christianity and Hinduism. The general trend in independent India is that the tribal people be assimilated in the Indian society to such an extent that their entity is completely lost. There are sociologists who have specifically ted that the solution of all tribal problems, economic, social as well as cultural, is in complete assimilation in to the Hindu society. There are anthropologists, on the other hand, who put forward their scheme of national parks, that is to say, complete non-interference in tribal people. According to them the tribal people should join to develop on the lines of their choice. Those who stand for upset assimilation of the tribal society into Hindu society forget the people have their own cultural tradition and complete assimilation not is quite useful, in fact, it may cause great injury to them. But cultures have some aspects and facts which should be preserved ill costs; in fact, some of them might prove useful and desirable the rest of the country. This is also hundred per cent true for the widow of tribal society in general and the Santhal tribe in particular.

In Santhal society, in spite of Modernizing forces operating, the important role of its traditional culture is still in popular in the management of cares of the aged caring is tackled by family intervention. These days, with the growth of population, condition of insecurity in maintaining a large family and above all, spread of modern education, growth of urban centers, a situation has arisen which has offered varied occupational pursuits and, as a consequence, people have become out of their narrow environs. As a result, in many cases problems have become acute through various interactional phases. Naturally, therefore, condition of old aged woman, especially the conditions of the widows have become unenviable and this indicates the necessity of studying their cases which has been done in this chapter from a close range. Due to old age, different age related changes are found among the Santhal widows' physiology. Regarding vision problem majority of the age widows have no such problem. Few of them are the victims of diminishing visual ability. About 50 per cent of the aged widows are suffering from cataract but very few have undergone eye operation. Those who have lost more than half of their teeth are facing gastro-intestinal problem. Few Santhal widows are suffering from other physical problems such as hearing problem, skeletal problem, breathing problem, nervous system problem, skin problem, kidney problem etc., but they are not getting proper treatment and care due to their poor socio-economic condition. The most common difficulty among them is poor eye-sight and impaired hearing capacity. Thus, the aged widows suffer from one or more physical problems but majority of them are capable to undertake certain personal tasks without the assistance of others. During the illness the family members provide help and co-operate them at any time. They get more help from their daughters. Old age is characterized by economic insecurity, ill health, loneliness, resistance to change and failing mental and physical power. They become weak even than they remain busy in domestic works. The widows have to face economic problems either due to their insufficient income or no income at all. During economic crisis they are not in a position to fulfill their needs and desire. This automatically creates so many socio-psychological problems among them. It has been found that the Santhal widows have some socio psychological problems. Very few widows have reported that they are getting almost all support from their family members so they do not live under pressure where are majority of them are not happy with the fully support from their families. They keep themselves busy in household work more than male even than they feel more isolated than the males. They also complain that they no more get the same kind of treatments from their family members as they used to get during their young age. Some of them feel themselves as social burden for their respective families. The few widows of joint families are always under the pressure of various forms of social problems, such as, lack of involvement in decisionmaking process and social participation, unrespectable behaviour and conflicting relationships with younger generations. Tension is greater in joint families has also been reported by Saraswati (1985). They are also facing the problem of generation gap to a considerable extent. The opinions of the aged widows are generally not recognized by the younger generation. In this way we find that after losing their husbands they face the problem of loneliness. Even those who are under the joint families are also facing this problem of loneliness. Many more problems are related to the economy. If the economic crisis will be solved than most of the other problems would be automatically solved. Economic insecurity is the main corroding problem of the aged widows.

The Planning Commission, Government of India has put down the following conditions for providing the financial support to organisation: (i) it must be a registered society under Registration of Societies Act 1860; (ii) it must not be linked directly or indirectly to any political party and any one holding public office through a process of election is not qualified to represent voluntary agencies, (iii) it must be based in rural area and should have worked there for at least four or five years, (iv) it must have professional and managerial expertise to produce regular and audit statements and report for funds received from the government, (v) it is explicitly connected to secularism, socialism and democracy, it must declare that it will adopt only legal and non-violent means for rural development purposes, and (vi) it must implement antipoverty, minimum needs and socio economic development programmes designed to raise awareness among the families living below the poverty line and leading to an improvement in the quality of their lives. The problem of social and economic amelioration of Harijans, Adivasis and other weaker communities is so vast that it cannot be tackled by government alone. After independence many voluntary organizations have began to introduce the provision of development services like health, education, agriculture, irrigation, drinking water, economic activities etc. More recently they are mainly concerned with the issues of deforestation, air and water pollution, ecology, rights of women, rights of construction workers, occupational health and safety, land degradation and alienation, housing rights, right to information and work, adult literacy and education of women, problems of the aged and their welfare etc. The voluntary organisations are people's own organizations and are accountable to the society in which they are mainly concerned for the work. The government, both the central and states have recognized the importance of voluntary action. Sachchidanand has rightly pointed out that the voluntary bodies have a role in creating a welfare state. It is human institution designed by human beings to meet human needs and their members must be active men and women. They are independent of statutory authority and their policy is framed and controlled by their own members. It represented the organized expression of the people's urge for social change. Shri Jayprakash Narayan held that the voluntary action could produce better and faster results if it was backed by resources both human and material. It was believed that both government and non-government agencies are complementary to each other rather than competitive. With the good result and constructive works the voluntary organizations have been widely recognized from national and international sources.

The Government's First Plan document says" A man or responsibility for organizing activities in different fields, of social welfare like the welfare of women and children, social education, community organisation etc. falls naturally private voluntary agencies. These agencies have long been working in their own humble way and without adequate aid for the achievement of their objectives with their own leadership, organisation and resources. Any plan for social and economic regeneration should take into account the services rendered by these agencies and the State should give them maximum co-operation is strengthening their effort. Public co-operation through voluntary social services organisation is capable of yielding valuable results in canalizing private efforts for the promotion of social welfare. In the Seventh Five year Plan Document it was clearly mentioned that voluntary organizations can supplement government effort so as to offer the rural poor choices and alternatives. It is, thus, necessary that in the years to come, serious efforts have to be made to involve the various voluntary agencies in development programmes particularly in the planning. If the economic crisis will be solved than most of the other problems would be automatically solved. Economic insecurity is the main problem of the aged widows.

In Bihar a large number of voluntary organizations are functioning in different socio-economic sectors. Even then Bihar is comparatively having lesser voluntary organizations than other states of India. There were few voluntary organisations in the area of tribal Bihar such as Santlial-Pahariya Seva Mandal, It was the Jai Prakash Movement which gave new direction to voluntary action in Bihar and in the country as a whole. Jai Prakash inspired the youths through his new vision. He gave then not only a ray of hope but also an agenda of action which could be put in to operation through individual or group effort. Thus, voluntary action received a great spurt in Bihar. The wave of establishing voluntary organisation has reached in Giridih and other districts too since last two decades. Important among them are Institute of Rural Management, Badlao Foundation, People's Institute for Development and Training, Prerna Bharati, Judav, Lokjagritikendra, Nehru Yuva Kendra etc. There organizations are actively engaged for the improvement of socio-economic conditions of the Santhal. This is an accepted phenomenon that tribal situation is going at rapid transition. There are several factors responsible for it. The changes occur in two ways one is due to the voluntary borrowing and the other due to the pressure of outside force. Voluntary borrowing takes place

Scheduled Tribes: The Introduction

The brahmin who flies into a rage atthe touch of a mahar - that's no Brahmin. The only absolution for such a Brahmin is to die for his own sin.

When it fulfills people's interest and it is constantly in their consciousness. But in other case, a situation of need and pressure is applied to compel the people for the changes.

The Scheduled Castes and Ad or Adi-dharmi

During the 1920s, a section of the Chamar, the Chuhra castes in particular, and other untouchable castes in general, claimed to be Ad Dharmi in an effort to project a joint front. Ad Dharam was indeed a political extension of the Ravidas Sabha and was based on an ideology that untouchables belonged to a quom, which is a first or primeval (Adi) faith (Dharm); these were later made to become Hindus under the during of immigrant Aryans. Ad Dharm was recognized as a religion during the 1931 census, which recorded a population of 418,789 Ad Dharmis, representing one-tenth of all untouchables in Punjab Juerie next two decades the movement petered out and the Ad Dharm Mandal was subsequently merged with Dr Ambedkar Scheduled Castes Federation in the late 1940s (Sabarwal, 1976). It may be concluded that the Bhils had their own political organisation based on their democratic values. The invaders tried to break their organisation but could not succeed. The British efforts of breaking tribal organisation began in 1818. The Bhils fought a long struggle to protect their organisation during the British period and ultimately they could not save that and finally in independent India their age old organisation came to an end.

Bhils Family Structure

The family was the smallest unit of social organization among the Bhils. The kiths and kins lived nearby to each other in a group locally known as kutumb. But at the same time it was based on individual freedom and did not represent the caste Hindu joint family system in any way. The Bhil family consisted of the male head, his wife or wives and unmarried children. When a Bhil son married he got separated from his parents and established a new home (hut) in the pal. In fact the separation was neither asked by the son nor was trusted upon by the father but it was a healthy common customary tradition among them. The separation was not complete in all respects but only a separate hut and a piece of land was allotted to him where he could manage his living and subsistence independently. This system on the one hand fostered a proper maturity and on the other avoided the burdensome dependency. Again the separation was semi-economic and semi- social to some extent. The elders were obeyed and honoured by the younger in the family. Though, the Bhil society was male dominated but the women enjoyed more freedom and respect. In the social and community matters joint decisions were taken in the family though the decisions taken by the head of the family or elders in some emergency or unavoidable circumstances was owned by the all family members. The separation among the Bhil families was cordial and harmonious which was a source of strength to their social system. It was never alike the caste Hindus where separation lead to enmity among the brothers. Final separation and partition of property took place after death of head of the family._The family functioning was based on customs and traditions of the community. In case of any dispute the family matters were also referred to the community 'Panchayat.' Thus, the family matters were not only individual concern; rather they were the community affairs too.

Marriage System

Contemporary British sources reveal the marriage system of the Bhils by appreciating as follows: It is clear that child marriages were not prevalent among the Bhils. The tribe, though not absolutely so, was considered as one endogamous group, but those who lived in the hills did not usually intermarry with those who resided in the plain, though this was not actually prohibited. On the other hand, the law of exogamy was strictly observed, i.e. a man might not marry within his own clan or gotra or within two degrees of his maternal and paternal relations; nor was marriage permitted among persons believing in the same goddess, known as the gotra devi, but as a rule each clan or group has its own goddess. There were various forms of marriages prevalent among the Bhils. Marriage by elopement was one of the popular forms. This method also had many forms from milder to strong. In case an unbetroth girl when eloped with some young man, her father and brothers just after knowing the pal where she had gone, attacked and burnt the seducer's house or, if unable to do so, burnt any house in the pal which might be handy. This was most probably resented and retaliated, and the quarrel might be prolonged, but sooner or later a panchayat was appointed to settle the dispute and compensation was awarded to the girl's father. A hole was dug in the ground and filled with water; the girl's father and the man she eloped with each dropped a stone into it and the incident was closed. After that the marriage rites were performed. In other form an unbetroth girl refused to elope when asked to do so, the man generally shouted in the village that he has taken so-and so's daughter's hand. On such occasion a panchayat assembled and the girl was generally handed over on payment of double the sum that had been awarded had she originally consented to elope. The other form was crossing the River (Nadi Par Karna) in which young boy and girl when agreed to marry they might had gone to the other bank of the river by crossing it they were recognized as married. If the father of girl caught them before crossing the river then marriage could not take place and the matter was again settled by the Panchayat. In this form *dapa* (Marriage expenses) was paid. **Kalai Pakadna**or holding the wrist was another form in which when agreed boy held girl's wrist on the occasion of some fair, festival or ceremony and matter was disclosed to the parents. The marriage took place with the consent of both the parents in usual manner. If some dispute arose the matter is settled by the Panchayat.

Marriage by abduction was also prevalent. In some cases the betrothed girl was entered in the house of bridegroom without marriage which was known as "*Aie Pesvu*". This happened when there was an extraordinary delay in the marriage. Ghar Jawai or **service marriage** was a very simple form of marriage in which a marriageable boy did not have the money to pay**dapa** he used to live with the girl's father and disposed the agricultural and cattle breeding work with him for some time. During this stay his friendship with the girl was converted into husband-wife relationship. The Bhils enjoyed full freedom in selecting their life partners. **Ata-Sata** was the marriage by exchange of sisters by two young men. It is said that such type of marriage was done when both the parties did not have money to pay for **dapa** (Marriage expenses) and had sisters for exchange. This version is not fully correct. In fact it was not possible to all to have love-affairs which could be materialized and also all could not get the offer or proper offer for their boys and girls in normal course used this form of marriage. Normal marriage with proposal from boy's side was known as **Hadi** which was much in vogue among the Bhils of plains. Betrothal customs: Betrothal took place before the girl was arrived at a marriageable age. The father of the girl could himself take no steps for his daughter's marriage; were he to do so, suspicion was aroused that there was something wrong with her. The proposal for the girls had come from the suitor or his father or other relative and it was open to the girl's father to accept it or not. If he considered the match suitable, he discussed the matter further and the dapa was settled; the amount was said to vary between Rs. 30 and Rs. 50. In Jodhpur, however, the dapa was the sum paid to the Darbar or the Jagirdar or the Panch or tribal council (as the case may be) for permission to celebrate the marriage. Thereafter the Sagai or betrothal ceremony took place. The custom in Mewar (Udaipur) was to place the girl on a stool under which six pice were thrown; a rupee, a pice and a little rice were put in her hand and she threw them over her shoulder. In Banswara the boy's father made a cup of the leaves of the dhak tree and, placing on the top of an earthen pot of liquor, put inside it two annas in copper coin; the girl's brother or some other boy among her relations, took the money and turned the cup upside down: The betrothal was then complete and it only remained for the assembled company to drink the liquor. The dapa was usually paid between the betrothal and the date fixed for the marriage, half in cash and half in kind. The custom of dapa has been described as the bride price by the British authors and the Indian authors copied it which is a wrong notion.

Jodhsingh Mehta has mentioned two type of dapa i.e. of sixteen and of Fourteen and quarter. He has also related the dapa with the quality of feast given by the father of bride to the Barat and the community members who assembled in the marriage ceremony. In fact dapa has been never a source of income to bride's father. An author of present time writes "The bride price in cash is usually a modest sum amounting to no more than a few hundred rupees. There is nothing here to gladden the hearts of a girl's parents as the sum will only partly meet the expenses of marriage." Their marriage ceremonies were quite interesting. Just after payment of dapa ceremonies and rejoicing began several days before the wedding. A doll of clay, called *dardi*, pierced all round with needles, was placed in the house of the bridegroom; it was perhaps intended to represent the Bhil the typical archer armed cap-a -pie with arrows, on the day of the wedding. The bridegroom, having been well anointed with pits (a mixture -of turmeric, flour, etc.) and wearing the peacock's feather was proceeded to the bride's house accompanied by his friends and relatives. At the borders of the village he was met by the bride's father who performed the ceremony of tilak, and made the customary present of a rupee. On reaching the bride's house, the bridegroom had to strike the toran or arch erected for the purpose, with his sword or stick, and the arti was done before him by way of welcome. The actual marriage ceremony, at which sometimes a Brahman and sometimes an elderly member of the bride's family officiated, consisted in the young couple, the skirts of whose garments were tied together, sitting for some time with their faces turned to the east before a fire (Horn) or a lamp fed with ghee, and then joining their right hands took pheras round the fire four times. On the first three of these pheras (circuits) the bride took precedence, while the last was led by the bridegroom subsequently the bride was often placed on the shoulder of each of her male relatives in turn and danced about till exhausted. In the evening great feast was arranged which consisted of bread and goat's or buffalo's meat. Wine was freely used. In fact the belief was that without it there could not be a perfect ceremony but many times its reckless use caused riots, and instead of merrymaking there had been fighting. The married couple was provided with a separate hut for the night, while their relatives got drunk. On the following morning the bride's father gave his daughter a bullock or a cow or any worldly goods with which he might wish to endow her and after presenting the bridegroom's father with a turban, used to give him leave to depart. Polygamy is described by the British as well as by the Indian author that polygamy was prevalent among the Bhils. But it was not the polygamy akin to the Rajputs because it was done when the first wife was barren or seriously ill. The marriage of two sisters or more sisters with the same person was permissible. This was the case of social security not the immoral act. The natra or widow remarriage was also a cause of polygamy because in most of the cases the widow of elder brother was remarried with the younger brother irrespective of his marital status. This was again a matter of social security. Divorcees were also taken as wives by the married men. Fresh second marriages were not much in practice while the cases of widow and divorcee marriages concerned mainly the social security and these also avoided various immoral acts. Thus, the polygamy among the Bhils had a specific feature and it was a healthy social tradition.

Divorce

Divorces were allowed but were rare. A man wishing to divorce his wife, in the presence of some of his tribesmen torn her sari breadth wise, loudly proclaimed his intentions. He bound in the torn cloth at least one rupee and the garment were then returned to the woman who carried it about as the charter of her new liberties. In case a woman left his husband without a formal divorce and eloped with another man, the later had to pay a fine called *Jhagra* to her husband. Divorce was both way and reasons included barrenness, illness, cruelty, impotence, excommunication, poverty and misbehavior etc. Polyandry was prohibited among the Bhils.

Widow Remarriage

Widow remarriage was common among the Bhils; the ceremony was called ***natra or Karewa.*** On the death of an elder brother the next took his widow, but an elder brother could not take a younger's widow. She was either returned to her parents or found another husband in another gotra or clan. A detailed description is given in the Gazetteer of Udaipur State (Ajmer 1908, p. 240-41) as follows "After the funeral of a married man, his widow, if young, is asked by his relatives if she wishes to remain in her late husband's house or be married again; and if, as is usually the case, she wishes to be married again, she replies that she will return to her father's house. Should the deceased have left a younger brother, he will probably step forward and assert that he will not allow her to go to any other man's house, and then going up to her, will throw a cloth over her and claim her; he is, however not bound to take on his brother's widow, but it is such a point of honour that even a boy will usually claim the right. Similarly, the lady is not bound to marry her late husband's younger brother, but as a matter of fact she is almost always agreeable; if, however, she declines the match and subsequently marry someone else, the younger brother will probably burn down the latter's house and generally make himself objectionable until the usual panchayat intervenes and awards him some small sum as compensation for his disappointment. Should the deceased have left no younger brother, his widow returns to her father's house as soon as the period of mourning is over, and stays there till she can find another husband. No formal ceremony is requisite for a natra; the man takes a few clothes and drink etc, to the widow, usually on a Saturday night, they join hands, and their relations and clansmen eat and drink together."

Religion

The Bhils during the British period were classified as Animist. It is very difficult to say finally that which religion they observed because on the one hand they worshipped Hindu gods and goddesses and on the other they have their own deities. In addition to it they had their own philosophy regarding the human life. In the Imperial Gazetteer of India their religion is mentioned as follows: "The Animists are found in eleven States, and--are mostly Bhils and Girasias residing in the wild tracts in the south. They share the usual belief that man is surrounded by a ghostly company of powers, elements, and tendencies, some of whom dwell in trees, rivers or rocks, while other preside over cholera, small-pox, or cattle diseases, and all require to be diligently propitiated by means of offering and ceremonies. In which magic and witchcraft play an important role. In fact the religion of the Bhil was a mixture of Animism and Hinduism. They also worshipped the Hindu gods and goddesses but at the same time they did not believe in Brahminical priestly order. The Bhils had countless deities belonging to their family, clan, village or Pal community, natural activities etc. The Mata was a main deity and in addition Mahadeo, Parbati, Hanuman and Bhairon were their favourite deities. In the Hilly tracts of Mewar and Dungarpur they had great faith in the idol at the famous

Jain Temple of Rikhab Dev and called the god Kalaji Bapji from the colour of the image. Another popular local deity in Udaipur was Khagaldeo, probably a form of snake worship, while in the parts of Jodhpur the Bhils had shown much respect to Pabu and to the Kabirpanthi Sadhus. Gopaldeo (god of cattle), Kshetrapal (god of field), Himaryo (god of boundaries), Magra Baba (god of mountains) were also recognized as gods. Rivers, earths, sky, fire, air, sun and moon, various trees and grasses also came in the category of gods. The Bhils also believed in superstitions. They also religiously believed in witchcraft which was locally known as Dakan or Dakni or Chudel. There were bhopas in many of the large villages, whose duty was to point out the woman who caused the injury. The women identified as dakans were tortured a lot and were put to death in cruel manner. There has been also a tradition of religious reformers among the Bhils. One of the oldest Panth to be established in the Bhil country was the Baneshwar Dham Panth which had origin to a certain Mavji Maharaj. He was born probably in the first half of the 18th century. Another sect that has gained considerable following among the Bhils was Surmal Das Panth. It was named before Kheradi Surmal who gained popularity in the 1860s. In the first decade of the 20th century Govind Gin launched religious reform movement which culminated into a politico-economic struggle. In the same manner Motilal Tejawat also launched social reform movement which eventually took political colour.

Food and Drinks

The Bhils used very simple food. Shyamaldas writes that "these People get less maize, Jowar and barley but they get more Kuri, Codra, Mal and Shamlai (inferior millets) which is a junglee grain; in addition to these they feel pleasure in eating the boiled Mahuwa.", they eat wheat and rice and on festive occasions they took feast of buffalo or goat. They were fond of tobacco and much addicted to liquor, which was distilled from the flowers of the mahuaa or from the bark of the babul or from molasses. Honey and oats were also used in food, while Mango and plum were their favorite fruits. Fishes were also used in the food.

Language & Education

In 1908 Grierson wrote that the dialect of the Bhils known as 'Bhili' contained a number of non-Aryan words, some of which appear to come from the Munda and Dravidian language. But the Bhili spoken during the modern period was not akin to as identified by Griesson Father it was intermediate between Hindi and Gujarati. There were various dialects of the Bhili language such as Bhili, Wagdi and Grassia. Bhili and Wagdi were the vernaculars of Mewar, Uiswara, Kushalgarh, Dungarpur and Partabgarh; Grassia of Sirohi and Marwar; and Magra-ki-boli of the Merwara sub district of Ajmer-Merwara. The Bhils had not any formal system of education before the advent of the British. They used to learn various skills of archery, hunting, fishing, cultivation, cattle breeding etc. in practice from their elders. The Bhil had also their literary traditions in the form of folk songs and stories but all in oral or verbal. Educational status of the Bhils was measured in the census of 1901. The same has been described in the Gazetteer of the Udaipur State as follows: "Education is practically non-existent, but there are a few schools in Udaipur and Dungarpur at which Bhil children attend, and the recruits of the Mewar Bhil Corps are sent to the regimental school. The last census report does not give the number of literate Bhils, but tells us that only 340 Animists (307 males and 33 females) were able to read and write, and that one of them knew English. As more than ninety-one percent of the Animists were Bhils and the remainder became two distinct tribes due to different professions and habitations in different geographical conditions. There are many legends regarding the origin of the Minas which do not have any logical and historical basis but denote some meaning about the historicity of the Mina tribe. *There is a legend regarding the origin of the Minas. It is said that when Parshuram resolve to annihilate Kshatriyas from the earth, countless Kshatriyas took agriculture and animal husbandry to save themselves from slaughter. Whenever they were asked whether they were Kshatriyas they would invariably exclaim in reply "Mainna, Main Na", i.e. "I am not, I am not". This is how the Mina community is believed to have come into existence.*

The Minas themselves also claim their origin from the Matsya or Mina Avatara or the fish incarnation of Vishnu. Matsya and Mina are two names for a fish in Sanskrit. The tribe derived from Mina and the country consisting of the former princely states of Alwar, Bharatpur, Dholpur and Karauli in which the Minas abound was known as Matsya desh. They also trace their origin from the Vedic Kshatriias and cite the Vedic word mehna meaning prowess in support of their contention.

The above description is not sufficient to unearth the origin of the Minas. Though, there may be some other indigenous sources by which their origin could be known but these could not be discovered till now. Due to limitations of the present study, I could not concentrate on this particular issue. Even then efforts have been made to reach to some conclusion in this regard. The accounts of the British authors are biased. They have tried to confuse the real situation and alike the Bhils the descriptions about the Minas are not correct. For instance M.A. Sherring recorded that: 'The Meenas are said to be descended from those Rajputs who, in the wars between their own tribes, or between them and the invading Mahomedans, were corbelled to quit their native country, and to seek refuse in the fastness's of Rajputana, where they formed alliances with aboriginal families, abandoned many of their caste usages, and established new tribes". He further remarked: 'The Meenas of Jaypure and Udaypur onside themselves as superior in rank to all other Meenas, and consequently will hold no intercourse with them. In conclusion it may be said about the origin of the Bhil tribe that this was a homogeneous ancient tribe of India. The Bhils originated in India and from early forest life they developed their value based society during the centuries. Their evolution as a mankind took place in a long process alike the other races. They have their long and splendid history but at the same time tortuous and spiral too.

The mention of the adivasis is available in the ancient Indian Literature. They had been prominently mentioned in the epic literature but so far as Rajasthan is concerned, it may be said that prior to the Rajput conquest the Bhil tribe held a great deal of the southern and south-eastern of Rajasthan. The Bhils were overpowered by the Rajputs during 7th to 12th centuries. The Rajput invaders could not win over the Bhils finally but they succeeded in pushing the Bhils in the interiors of dense forests and mountains.

Thus, the Bhils could not come under the subordination of the Rajputs and both lived side by side in constant struggle with each other. But during the Mughal period the Rajput established friendly relations with the Bhils. In this regard to recognize the Bhils as original inhabitants of the area they were given the right to Rajtilak on the forehead of Rajput chief on their succession to the throne. The Rajputs also recognized the Bhilchiefs as independent and autonomous rulers of their areas. The Rajput Bhil cooperation emerged during the Mughal period was the result of the necessity of the Rajputs as the Bhils resisted the Mughal armies from time to time. During the Rajput-Maratha conflict the Bhils sided up with the Rajputs. Thus, the Bhils came into direct confrontation with the Marathas. The Marathas also attacked the Bhil pals (villages). During these attacks the Bhils were not helped by the Rajput States and they were left on the mercy of cruel plundering hordes of the Marathas. The Rajput states concluded treaties and agreements with the Marathas, while the Bhils remained in struggle with the Marathas and Pindaris. Thus, the Rajput-Bhil unity established during the Mughal period was shaken. In 1818 all the Rajput states of southern Rajasthan concluded treaties with the British. The British tried to bring the Bhils under strict political and administrative control which resulted in the revolt of Bhils. During the modern period the social political and economic organisations of the Bhils were traditional but were very strong.

I have conducted local survey of the Tribal people of Dadra and Nagar Haveli in the month of January, 2013.

The Assistance provided by Mrs. Sonal Pathak and Mrs. Arti Mishra of Red Cross. They conducted survey door to door under my guidance. They have examined the ladies and gentlemen from Adivasi Community. Their names and details are given in this book.

Sr. no.	Name	Fathers Name/ Husband Name	Age	Profession	Caste/ Sub-Caste
1	Naniben Patel	Magiyabhai Patel	70	House Wife	Hindu (Dhodia)
2	Vina Prajapati	Vaman Prajapati Purushottam Par	47	House Wife	Prajapati
3	Hanshaben Patel	Shankarbhai Patel Chandubhai Patel	45	House Wife	Hindu (Dhodia)
4	Chandubhai patel	Navalbahi patel	47	Govt. Servant	Hindu (Dhodia)
5	Danabhai Harijan	Natahabhai Harijan	50	Govt. Servant	Hindu (Harijan)
6	Sabita Dala Gavit	Dala Gavit (divorcee)	40	Veg. seller	Konkani
7	Dudhai Govind Musara	Govind Musara	55	Veg. seller & Agriculturist	Konkani
8	Jigneshbhai Patel	Jayantibhai Patel	25	Peon SMC	Hindu (Harijan)
9	Chanchalben Patel	Mangayabhai Patel	47	Housewife	Hindu (Dhodia)
10	Dhoniben Bhoya	Lakhubhai Bhoya	32	Housewife	Hindu (Konkani)
11	Dinesh Bablu Bara	Bablu Bara	25	Peon	-
12	Jani Raman Dhorabhoya	Raman Dhorabhoya	40	Housewife	Hindu (Konkani)

| 13 | Patilben Patel | Harikishan Patel | 62 | Housewife | Kambali Patel |
| 14 | Pitar Rama Choudhary | Rama Choudhary | 30 | Peon | - |

The latest survey enlightens the stages of life style of the people. The ceremonies of child- birth, language taught to child, engagement and marriage custom. Pre-marital and extra marital sex relation, monogamy, polygamy, divorce culture and widow remarriage, status of Ghar Jawai(service marriage) ways of acquiring mates, food and drink, religion, God, Goddess, and vows to God, faith in medical profession etc.

I would like to summarize the survey report that child birth ceremony is known "CHATTI". Their languages are Dhodia, Gujrati, Konkani, Marathi and Varli. The engagement and marriage custom performs by garlanding each other. Previously girl goes to the house of boy for marriage and stay there as known "UDHADI". They perform marriage in the day. They use bullock-cart for Barati. Nowadays it is replaced by motor vehicles. After marriage bride and bride-groom are separated by erecting separate hut near to their house. On next day to marriage bride is taken back to parent home, known as "AANU". In Gavit community children and parent perform their marriages at a time it is known "Nawara-Nawari". The engagement they refer as "Lagan nakki karyo", or "Chandala" or "Sakharpuda". In rare cases girl became mother first and then marry, as Naniben Patel told but nowadays the custom is not seen. There is no custom of extra martial sex relation. There is general practice of monogamy but there are rare cases of keeping two wives but not permitted in the existing law. Widows are allowed for re-marriage. The percentage of widow marriage in middle aged women is rare. The custom of Ghar Jamai is called "Khandhadiya". It is called, "service marriage". The ceremony called during pregnancy is known "Shrimant".

Their food is bread. It is prepared by rice, jowar, makka, wheat, nagali. They eat shark, fish, and chicken. They drink Bear, mahuwa, tadi, desi daru. They used to dance toor-tarpa and thali. They believe in God Shankar, Swami Narayan, Brahamdev, Ramdevgir, Konkani Maa and Pitrulok, Khwajagar, Nivaj, Mahalaxmi Mata. They wear Kanchado and Blouce, Saree. Now a day it is noted that villagers of Silvassa are attracting towards Christian religion and Swami Narayan. They are performing the marriage as per Swami Narayan Religion. They are attending Church to get cloth and Ghamchha. They have extreme faith towards, baba, zhadfuk, bhagat if they are suffering from diseases. Nowadays, they are availing medical facilities from Vinoba Bhave Civil Hospital and private Doctors. Dr. V.K. Das, Head of the Vinoba Bhave Civil Hospital rendering good services and devoting full time day and night in the Hospital. Dr. Chittapure and Dr. Mrs. Chittapure providing tired less service to the adivasi patients. Some time local people ignore the Hospital service and they scrummed to non-professional medical persons (Bhagat-Bhuva) and lost their lives. Tina an Adivasi girl of administration sent to work in my Bungalow in Tokarkhada, Silvassa, injured her left hand thumb. Because of pain she remained absent for 10 days. One morning she came on duty in my Bungalow. I saw her thumb appears tremendous big size and she is whipping. She took treatment from Baba. Who gave her many threads chanting mantras. I immediately took her in my Government car to Vinoba Bhave Civil Hospital Silvassa and met Dr. VatteKatte Das. He told it is too late and thumb suffers gangrene it should be cut otherwise poison goes other parts of body. Gangrene means decay of flesh. She was admitted in the hospital for 10 days and recovered. She joins her duty after discharge from hospital.

****